The MODERN GOD

The MODERN GOD

✝

FAITH

in a SECULAR

CULTURE

by Gustave Weigel, S.J.

The Macmillan Company, New York
Collier-Macmillan Ltd., London

Imprimi potest
    Joannes M. Daly, S.J.
    Praep. Prov. Marylandiae
Nihil obstat
    Edward A. Cerny, S.S.
    Censor Librorum
Imprimatur
    ✠ Lawrence Joseph Shehan, D.D.
    Archbishop of Baltimore
    September 26, 1962

The Macmillan Company, New York
Collier-Macmillan Canada, Ltd., Galt, Ontario
Divisions of The Crowell-Collier Publishing Company

Library of Congress catalog card number: 63-12138
Printed in the United States of America
Designed by Mary A. Brown

PREFACE

Goucher College in Baltimore honored me in 1961 with an invitation to give the Elmore B. Jeffery Lectures. This invitation I accepted, and I called the lectures: "Faith in a Shaky World." In 1962 Northwestern University similarly invited me to give the Shaffer Lectures of that year. There I gave the series under the title: "God: Dead or Alive?" To both institutions for their gracious hospitality I am grateful. In particular I wish to thank Professor Edmund Perry who was my solicitous guardian angel at Evanston.

The Goucher Lectures are reproduced in this volume in the first three chapters and the next three chapters represent the lectures given at Northwestern. The general theme of both series is the place of God in modern culture. For that reason I have supplemented the lectures with other meditations I have recently made on the same theme. I hope this will give me an excuse for some repetition which the reader will surely find in the following pages.

Gustave Weigel, S.J.
Woodstock College

CONTENTS

I.

FAITH

in a SHAKY

WORLD

1. *The* MILITANCY *of* FAITH

The general title for this section of the book includes the term "shaky world." The phrase is not intended to refer to the physical earth we all live on. That has been shaky since the earliest moment of its evolution and the seismologists can give us startling data concerning the high mobility of the floor of our common home. The world which is the background of our concern is not the material stage on which we move but rather the sociological setting in which we live our lives.

Nor do we mean by faith something exclusively religious. Every religious fellowship rests on some faith, but other types of social union do too. We call the total world view of an organized political group its culture and at the root of every culture there is a faith. This faith is a stance toward the totality of reality. As a rule it is not expressed in systematic completeness, and many people who actually share in the faith are quite unatten-

3

tive to the faith which operates in them. The dynamic kernel of the total faith is theological, though by this word I do not wish to state that it is religious in the narrower sense of that word. It is theological because it has some idea as to the nature of the ultimate. Generic positivism and its specific variant, Communism, rest on a theology no less than do religions, because no man can escape the innate concern about the last things which are always the first things. If the translation of this concern is in churchlike terms, we can call the vision religious; if it spurns or ignores cultic symbolism, we can only call it merely theological. Aristotle, who shows little piety in his writings, still called his first or basic philosophy theological, and he was quite right. When the Greek used the word *Theos* (the operative root in the term theology), he did not necessarily mean any one of the gods whom he knew in his mythologies and worship. He could also understand the last dimension of reality as it swims into man's ken.

That dimension is not open to experimental observation. It is the object of an apperception which accompanies man's every perception. In philosophy this phase of reality can be considered without any reference to the holy. Perhaps we can then make a distinction of importance. The divine is the absolute, unconditioned, ultimate bed of the real, while God is the same reality considered as the object which men call the holy. No world vision is possible without a theological commitment, though such a vision need not be prayerful, which is another way of saying religious.

The way I am using the word "faith" employs the term in its most general meaning. That there is a world beyond my own consciousness is a faith, animal faith, as George Santayana calls it. Only in consciousness do we find the world; never in itself. This fact makes idealism always possible, and even probable in those cultures which give great value to the individual person. Faith, as I use the word, merely gives assent to a proposition for which there is no unambiguous experimental evidence. In this rough way it lives up to the definition of faith which we find in the Epistle to the Hebrews (11.1) whereby faith gives substance to what we hope for and serves as an irrefutable argument for things unseen.

For the sake of illustration let us consider the most atheistic form of theology, the philosophic stance called materialism. Such a philosophy does not deny the existence of an ultimate dimension of reality. It cannot be *that* atheistic. It simply denies that the ultimate transcends the constitution of the observable universe. Yet it conceives the nucleus or matrix of the universe to be a pattern of cosmic power from which all things flow and which dominates absolutely all events in the world. This power pattern must be studied, for only in this way can we use cosmic power to the satisfaction of our own desires. This basic power-drive creates all, directs all, dominates man and all that concerns man. There is no prayerful recognition involved in this faith. It can indeed accept the phrase from the Lord's Prayer, "thy will be done," not as a wish but as a cold statement of fact. But materialism effects a change in the modality of the expression. It is completely indicative, and not optative. If "thy" is considered equivalent to "its," then the formula comes to say that the drive of basic power is inexorable. In this form the prayer is quite congenial to the materialist. Lucretius in his great dissertation on the materialistic structure of all reality kept a place for the gods, but they, no less than man, were subject to the unavoidable dominion of atomic power. For Lucretius the gods were not divine. Divinity was the impersonal agent operative in moving atoms.

Neither Lucretius, nor his antecessor, Epicurus, could produce a common faith in classical culture. The people did not accept their materialism. Neither Lucretius nor Epicurus had the will or the means to impose their view of reality on their communities. Hence the Graeco-Roman culture was never as materialistic as men like Democritus, Epicurus and Lucretius desired. They remained to the end of classical culture alien voices in a community that tolerated but did not follow them. Religious worship and practices were highly regarded in Graeco-Roman culture. Without ever becoming a clear theory, divinity in Rome and Greece never was so restricted as in the Lucretian vision. The unarticulated theology of the ancients formed a culture which was much less than exclusively positivistic.

A cohesive community is not made up by sheer numbers joined together by physical contact. It springs out of a culture which produces the community and through its production becomes gradually reproduced and changed itself. At the root of every culture there is a theology, implicit or explicit. The systematic and logical expression of such a theology is the fruit of the reflections of thinkers, but no such elaborated system actually photographs the living theology of the community. This theology is not so precise nor so logical as the abstraction derived from it by the theorists. But the theory and the existential reality all point to a faith commonly accepted by the community in its cooperative efforts to live a human existence. Government may be seized by willful groups who function in terms of a theology not accepted by the community as a whole. The result is tyranny with two possible consequences. Either the tyrannical minority may with time communicate its faith to the general public which then will have changed its culture, or the minority will lose its own faith and gradually adjust to the stubborn culture of the community at large. You cannot tell antecedently which of the two events will occur, because at any given moment both sides of the struggle adjust to each other in many subtle ways whose significance is hard to ascertain.

Up to recent times the coexistence of antagonistic cultures on our little earth was not only possible but a fact. Man's restricted capacity of movement with the concomitant need of satisfying his needs in terms of local possibilities necessarily circumscribed cultures within regional boundaries. Islam had its boundaries beyond which it could not heavily influence the culture of other groups. Tibet was a walled-in community, neither moving out of its fastnesses nor subject to the movement of others into its own domain. Tsarism did not actively modify the community of Western Europe. All these different ways of life, or cultures, were antagonistic to each other, but they were regionally encysted. Conflict was real only in the border areas. Far from the borders the Turk was no threat to the Europeans nor was the European a threat to the Tibetan.

Today the situation has changed completely. Whether we like it or not, we are becoming a one-world community in which the antagonism of cultures is making living together most precarious. A tribal war in the Congo did not disturb the denizens of England in the early nineteenth century any more than English-French strife bothered the Congolese, who didn't even know about it. In our time this is not so. We know only too well that Congolese disturbances affect the lives and hopes of Belgians, Americans, Russians and Syrians, few of whom have ever seen the Congo or want to. A *coup d'état* in Nicaragua during the nineteenth century was considered comic opera by Americans and Europeans. But not now. Such an action today becomes a grave preoccupation for men in Washington, London and Moscow.

8

Our shaky coexistence makes every new shake a threat to all. This explains the general malaise in the whole world. The nostalgic gaze backward excites modern man to seek for the security of peace. Actually this means that every community wants to live unthreatened in its own way according to its own vision of the good life. The strong French tendency toward neutralism is only an external aspect of the Frenchman's desire to be French in the historical way of the culture which developed him and which he in turn developed. He doesn't want to live in the Russian way nor in the American way. It may be a fact that current conditions do not give the Frenchman the possibility of rejecting the other two ways, but this of course neither he nor anybody else can see with shattering clarity. French faith in the French way will be stronger than the ambiguous evidence that a change is inevitable.

Men and women in our times are not reconciled to the instability of our political world. The constant alarms of tocsins to drop whatever the citizen is doing in order to man the walls against an aggressor hampers the evolution of a free life; one of the great four Rooseveltian freedoms is freedom from fear. Fear, and especially in its extreme form of panic, constricts human effort. It is painful and frustrating. We all want a peace as stable as the abiding human condition can allow. From the near and distant pasts we know that greater stability is possible and therefore we feel that our human craving for more stability is not unreasonable.

9

From this feeling very concrete dreams have come forth. Wendell Willkie's one world has now become a general persuasion. In terms of it, different visions of a unified world government have been proposed by minor seers and prophets. In fact, there are some people of great naïveté who think that because the idea is so good, any movement for its realization is equally good. The World Federalists in general need not be classed under this heading, but certainly some individuals in that fraternity must be so labeled. The movement has not been able to recruit large numbers and the association does not make a deep impact on our thinking here or abroad. In fact, there are some Americans who consider the whole thing an essentially vicious phenomenon because of their own monolithic devotion to the American way.

The best current realization of the one-world idea is, of course, the United Nations Organization. And everyone must admit that its action in recent history has been beneficent. If it has not done all that modern man wants, at least it has reduced the dangers contained in our explosive situation. Champions of the United Nations point with pride to the relative success of their union, reminding us that perfect success is not to be expected on our earth which contains so much perversity even in the best of men.

Their observations make good sense to the average man. Certainly Americans by and large believe in the

United Nations. What they desiderate is that it be more effective than it is. When they are asked how this greater efficacy is to be achieved, they are reduced to stuttering vagueness. The concrete realities of our world just make utopian schemes somewhat pathetic.

It is quite clear to any man who knows no more about the United Nations than what is communicated to us by our organized press that the lack of total efficacy in the United Nations Organization stems from conflicts of interest of the member nations who make up the union. Americans cannot help but suspect that the Soviets are trying to make of the federation an instrument of their effort to conquer the whole world. The Russians certainly think that the Americans want to make the international structure a weapon whereby they can defend their own view of life. I suppose that both sides are right. In fact, I cannot see how they could be wrong. Communists in accord with their faith take it for granted that the good state for all the world is the Communist system. Our American allegiance to democratic freedom based on the right of the inviolability of individual opinion and communication makes us spontaneously reject the heavy authoritarianism of the Communist scheme. Even if it were granted that both sides are willing to follow their own faith with a spirit of tolerance for the other party, the push given by either party would be in opposition to the other. The two world views are in opposition by inner logic, and the men who follow the differing views cannot help but produce human oppositions in social and political contexts.

What then are we to do? It is not my purpose to answer this question because I do not have the sufficient knowledge or the proper training to achieve it. What I would like to do is to point out where the problem, practical as it is, seems to be situated.

Before we do this, we must consider certain solutions already offered. No man in his right senses thinks that all we have to do is bring together the representatives of the conflicting cultures into a conversation of sweet reasonableness. Given the differing faiths which are the bedrocks of culture, what is reasonable to one party in the dispute is utterly unreasonable to the other. By reasoning together, the best to be expected is compromise. This device can settle a concrete problem here and now, but the basic abiding conflict is untouched. Hence the instability remains, and it is the instability which is the real disease.

Another solution presents itself readily to the mind. Let one community, say the American, so increase its power that it can impose its will on all the others. The Roman Empire, which was the confederation of many nations and many cultures, was constructed in this way. Its great fruit was the *Pax Romana*, the Roman peace which prevailed in the Mediterranean basin for over three hundred and fifty years. The Roman governors were, by and large, tolerant of local folkways. In their own capital, Greek, the language of an absorbed people, actually was more prevalent than the native Latin for about a century. Within the boundaries of the Empire, there was no war for over three hundred years. Military action was only for police purposes within the commonwealth and for defense of the border. Great freedom was given to the inhabitants of the Roman world. This is a shining example of how a federation can come into being and work with a high degree of success.

Whatever we say about the Roman Empire, we must yet recognize certain facts. The *Pax Romana* had a black side to it. Tacitus puts into the mouth of the Briton, Galgacus, the assertion that the Romans made a wasteland and called it peace. (*Solitudinem faciunt et pacem appellant.*) Government moved out of the control of the people and was the prize of ambitious men, ruthless in their achievement of power. Corruption of every kind—in civic action, artistic and scientific production, general morality and interpersonal relations —gradually rotted away the Roman fiber.

Besides, can any national community today accumulate so much power that it could dominate all the peoples of the world? Atomic energy is a fearfully powerful auxiliary but it is at the disposal not only of one but of many nations. Then, too, does any nation have sufficient resolution to attempt so colossal a task as world domination? Perhaps, but certainly the people of the United States at present are not so resolved.

However, the solution to the problem of our present shakiness is not really a matter of physical power. If cultures are in conflict, the radical conflict is in faith. Every culture rests ultimately on its faith in a definite world vision. Such a faith is undoubtedly an intellectual achievement but there is a strong element of will behind the intellectual assent. There is no faith where there is no will to believe. An easy faith, which is no more than a readiness to accept the community's vision of reality as drawn up in some past time, will not put iron into a people. A faith to be dynamic must be ardently shared by the whole collectivity. It is difficult to measure the intensity of faith in a people. When times are good and life is easy, faith is not tested. It is in crisis and hardship that the caliber of faith is evident. It is faith that moves mountains, a feat today less impressive than the endurance of stretched-out suffering. Faith has as one of its meanings, steadfastness. To be steadfast to vision is the mark of strong faith. Is there anywhere in the world a people with unshakeable faith? That is the question. Such a nation will have the spiritual power to bring about a calming of the storm. I doubt if there is any student of current affairs who would dare say that any one people is today dedicated to the faith which such a people publicly professes. The written expressions of faith must not be identified with the faith actually living in the individuals.

During the sixteenth century Protestant Reformers launched the cry that by faith alone is man saved, but though they denied the salvific potentiality of works, they insisted that true faith will inevitably bring forth good works. They were talking religiously but their observation was good for faith in the larger sense. Perhaps a better formulation of the Reformers' slogan was that good works without faith were sterile. This ultimate sterility of works not rooted in faith is precisely what makes it so difficult to evaluate the works of any people at any given moment. One must see whether the works, seemingly good, are really faith in operation. A flash in the pan may be splendid but it is not a steady enduring light.

It seems to me, no trained observer and a mere armchair historian, that the one thing weak in our time is faith. Once more I must insist that I do not restrict faith to religious faith alone. I include the faith of the Communists, which certainly is not admittedly religious, but at best quasi-religious. Nationalism is a faith but it is very brittle. The national gods are always so small and they have not the greatness to make great men. As a result, a thoroughgoing nationalism can at most produce spurts of action and feeling. In the long run, it loses its power to direct the efforts of men. Nationalism is preva-

15

lent in our world, but we can consider it only as a sign of little faith. The nation is not ultimate and its gods are demigods of restricted creative power. The nations which have done much with their power have not made their gods in the image of themselves but they have believed that they themselves were the instruments of the great deity which is the full power at the heart of all things, man and his destiny included.

It seems to me that our restlessness and malaise manifest the absence of an overpowering faith anywhere in the world. There is no doubt that many faiths are soliciting our adhesion but none shines forth strongly enough to win the world's allegiance. In matters of religion, this is certainly evident. In spite of great efforts to revitalize the known religions, not one of them can muster the strength which flowed through the Arabs in the seventh and eighth centuries, which drove them from the deserts of Arabia to the Pillars of Hercules and to the frontiers of China, establishing in the lands of their conquest their language, their customs and their faith. Perhaps Buddhism, being pacifist, cannot dynamize the martial instincts always working in the mass of men. Judaism is too ethnic to attract the loyalty of those who are not of the Jewish people. Christianity is no longer one faith but rather a common label for over three hundred faiths. We know that great energy is being expended in our time to fuse the many churches into one, but one wonders at times if this very effort is not a sign of diminished faith rather than of faith in resurgence. It is unwise to say that religion is now only a minor force in man's total action. The religious prophet may arise at any time and call the people to ardent faith. Although this is so, it is equally so that there is no religious prophet on the horizon. One is tempted to say that no matter what faith might sweep over the nations, religious faith will only be absorbed into it rather than give it its specific form.

The faiths which are causing our instability are not religious. As we have seen, they are theological enough but their interest in divinity is only a search for power rather than a quest for the holy. There are many such faiths and all have adherents. Yet their hold on their own is not too strong and their quarrel with the others simply erects an atmosphere of world confusion in which we are whirling. We must remember that it is the very heart of any faith to see in its own vision the true structure of the ultimate. This is the true god and all the other gods are necessarily idols. Believers at every stage of history were horrified and disgusted with idolatry, anxious to destroy the idols which they considered demonic phenomena. Differing cultures must resolve their differences of theology before they can collaborate and coexist in harmony.

The difficulty of our time is that we are confronted with too many faiths, none of which is strong enough to energize a dominant portion of humanity which is

17

every day becoming more closely knit and more co-hesive. Militancy of faith is producing clash and chaos, but no victory.

If all these ideas be correct, at least in part, then it is clear that the problem facing all the peoples of the earth is theological. This certainly is the conclusion of the evidence I have mustered and the conclusion is certainly a proposition with which I concur. Arnold Toynbee seems to think that this is the abiding situation in all epochs of history. For him one generation under the stimulus of a prophetic figure of deep insight raises the human understanding of the divine. When this new level is reached universally or the new theology has exhausted its own resources, then a higher conception of divinity must rise out of the collapse of the previous faith and culture.

Without subscribing to Toynbee entirely, I certainly will go along with his basic insight. In our day we are worried about the atom bomb, the destructiveness of Communism, the threat of chaos rising from the advent of ancient peoples to take their place in the direction of terrestrial and cosmic affairs. We are menaced by economic and social disturbances by reason of the dazzling fruitfulness of scientific research. Change is of the order of the day, and the changes are so radical and so unforseeable that we have nothing secure in the structures which we have inherited from the wise men of the past. All these things are to be seen and felt. They are real enough nor are they delusions. However, they are only multiplicity which is meaningless unless we can see the unity in which they are rooted. If that one thing can be found, then we need not deal with the many branches that fan out from the source. We need deal with only that one thing and we have dealt with all.

My guess is that faith is too weak and too disparate in our moment. As a consequence our cultures are too weak and too disparate as well. Culture grows from faith and is specified by the faith which brought it forth. If this is the case, our task is to throw strong light on the theological foundations of these faiths. Faith cannot debate with faith because they have no ultimate common ground. Faiths can only rail at each other. Yet all are human things and we can analyze them. The acceptance of faith is a free act, and we cannot compel any man to believe one vision rather than another. However, we can show up the inadequacies of some faiths for the human situation. With this done, a given faith loses much of its recruiting power. This is the only task which seems possible and to it we shall dedicate two more of our meditations.

2. BRASH FAITHS *and* WEAK BELIEVERS

In the preceding chapter on the current confusion in the world we tried to see the relation between a people's faith and its cultural action. In this analysis we proposed an ancient idea, namely that every culture rests on a theology which in turn rested on a faith. By faith we did not mean only religious faith, which is commitment to the holy. Any world vision with a doctrine on the nature of the ultimate is a construction of faith, an assent of the mind to propositions not imperated by unambiguous evidence. The ultimate is beyond the observation of man and therefore it is reached in an inevitable apperception whose subsequent conceptual formulation produces an academic theology. Such a theology need not be religious because the ultimate in reality may not be conceived as the holy. The holy is the object of prayer

21

and when the ultimate is not prayerfully considered, theology is indeed at work but it is not religious. It is none the less dynamic and can give specification and energy to a world view.

We have also supported the idea that there are many cultures in conflict in our time and the conflict is painful for all men on our earth, because today it is impossible to restrict a culture to any one region. We have become a one-world community and the different cultures affect the whole world because they make portions of the totality act in disaccord with others. Collaboration and coexistence are rendered difficult by the diversity of cultures and the theologies embedded therein. Our frustrations and fears, so prominent in our moment, are ultimately based on this fact. The solution is either to achieve a common faith or to make one faith so strong that the others cannot prevail against it.

It is time that we look at the faiths guiding the efforts of man. Perhaps it is not too foolish to say that between 1750 and the decline of the old Roman Empire, the faiths which moved mankind were religious faiths. Before the nineteenth century, Islam was still an affirmation of the Koran and on principle the Muslim settled their problems in accord with its teaching. The Turkish sultan was not only a ruler over an empire but also the head of a religion which as such enjoyed priority in his concerns. The Tsar of the Russias was not only a temporal autocrat but also the defender of Orthodoxy, which was supposed to affect the last word in all his decisions. In the West, Christian doctrine in varying forms was the recognized normative principle for political resolutions. The kings and princes professed to make their policies under the judgment of the Gospel.

Needless to say, neither Turk nor Christian prince actually lived up to his profession and there was constant conflict between church and state. Yet in principle religious faith was supposed to be predominant in the conduct of statal affairs. For the West, the rationalism of the Enlightenment gradually became a new faith and by 1800 it was strong enough to be the foundation of political action. In the nineteenth century it became positivistic but it did not lose its basic theology which conceived the ultimate to be a cosmic power, completely immanent in our universe and quite impersonal in its being. Positivism merely substituted empirical observation for the Enlightenment's reasoning in its approach to the absolute. In our day Christian statesmen, Muslim leaders, Hindu political guides and Buddhist heads of state do not solve their problems in the political order with a reliance on their religious faiths, which are now relegated to the private and inner life of individuals. Governors do not appeal to this kind of faith, and when they take it into account, it is only because its presence is a public fact but not a functional norm. In one culture, the Russian, religion is not considered at all except as an unwelcome fact which in theory should gradually wither away.

After the French Revolution, in all the dominant

faiths a generic theology is accepted. Reality is identified exclusively with the observable structure of the universe. There is nothing real beyond it. The ultimate, and therefore divinity, is the patterned power at the heart of cosmic evolution. It is impersonal and inexorable. Today we are not so crude in our understanding of this reality. It is not identified only with physical force in the sense of the physicists' description of matter and motion. The core power of the universe produces thought and it permits freedom of action in the cosmos. A phase of the action of cosmic power is the free choice of men. Human purpose is a factor of evolving the universe, but in itself is only an actualization of the prime force spontaneously operative everywhere and in all things. To find out just what the structure of basic power is, man must observe. By trial and error he makes provisional mental constructions that will guide him in his own attempts to create and reshape reality. The scientific method of observation joined to the rationalization of the observed is considered the only valid and useful way to use the mind. Nor is the mind any longer considered to be an uncommitted instrument of man. It too, like all things in the cosmos, is subject to the conditioning that history and psychological evolution impose on it. This mind does not really see anything; it can only order its own empirical perceptions into useful and pleasing patterns. Truth is no longer what is, but only a faithful report of human experience, rendered objective by the use of univocal symbols and signs.

Man is incurably moral. No matter where he got it from, he is interested in the rightness and wrongness of his actions. As the old saw says, there is honor even among thieves. The present culture, stuck as it is with an immanent ultimate energizing the contingent universe, cannot appeal to timeless and ideal structures of human action. Morality is reduced to general usefulness or esthetic harmony and is thus relative to a man's situation which is never the same in two different moments of his existence. Nothing is right or wrong in itself but only with reference to a historical context. If it fits harmoniously and usefully into the moment of history, it is good. If it does not, it is bad. The supposition of older cultures that certain actions were wrong always and by intrinsic essence is no longer accepted as true but merely as an unfortunate carry-over from the past.

Now such a theology can be consistently presented. There is nothing in the observable universe that will refute it. Of course there is nothing in the observable universe that will prove it, but this is no true weakness in the system, because it is ultimately a faith. Faith needs no proof and to be a faith, it rests on no proof. It can and should have an apologetic, an argument for the reasonableness of such a faith. It does have such an apologetic, and strangely enough it is the apologetic proposed by the gospels. By their fruits you will know them. A good tree does not bring forth bad fruit and a bad tree does not bring forth good fruit. An adequate name for this kind of theology is naturalistic secularism. It is prevalent all over the world and our most esteemed professors of knowledge and wisdom propose it as the scheme of life to our youth and to our statesmen.

But it would be false to say that this theology is universally accepted by the men and women of our time. In terms of their heritage from the past, much of the theology of the cultures, now no longer dominant, influences the thinking of our people. The theologies of other times latently influence the outlooks of our contemporaries. Religious faith and secular faith are mixed in modern man. He knows that the mélange is producing malaise but he stubbornly refuses to drop either the old or the new. The result is confusion in the individual and in society. Action proceeds from contradictory theological views and it should not be surprising that contradiction is a quality of our achievements. Let us prescind for the moment from the question whether contradiction is a sign of error and unreality, yet one thing is certain. Contradiction in word or work is a discomforting experience for man.

The discomfort for Americans is all the higher because in their relations with Communist governments they deal with an action not in disaccord with the basic theology of naturalistic secularism. No matter what the

Russian or the Chinese peoples think, their governments proceed on the theological basis that divinity is naturalistic and secular. They have no hesitations and no inner conflict. Their professed faith in this theology is thorough and complete. The schizophrenia of the West, which believes in the theology of naturalistic secularism and also in a transcendental absolute, unfits it to agree with the Communists and unfits it to disagree with them. The Communist is not at all bound by a morality deriving from absolute transcendence. In fact he is morally bound to ignore it as something unreal. He knows the divine will for man and he has made that will his own. When dealing with such a single-minded person, our own weakened faith makes us singularly vulnerable. The conversations will always be distressing to us because whenever anything like agreement is approached, we suddenly find out that the words we use mean something else for our partner in dialogue. Democracy for him means the dictatorship of the Communist Party while for us it is a denial of any kind of dictatorship. When the Communist claims to be a champion of the worker and the downtrodden, we find out that he does not care in the least what the worker actually wants. The Communist gets at man's wants not by asking man but rather by interpreting man's desires by Communist faith. Words get to be so Humpty-Dumptyish that utter amazement takes the place of understanding.

If conversations with the Communists are frustrating, the course of their actions is even more so. By Communist faith, the communization of the whole world is foreordained. It will not come about without human effort for its achievement, but even in determinism these efforts are nevertheless free. In freedom and reason they are chosen and constructed. Not every planned act will necessarily be successful, but from the total series, indefinite as it seems at the moment, Communism will inevitably emerge. Each act just makes universal Marxism a little bit closer. The Communist can afford to be patient. He is as sure of his goal as the old-time Calvinist was sure of his salvation.

In consequence, the Communist can change his tactics without the slightest inner inconsistency. The inner impulse to total conquest of the world pushes out into action in all directions. If the external world does not absorb the branch sent out from one point, a branch is sent out elsewhere. The failure of one outthrust merely facilitates the release of another outthrust. The non-Communist just cannot tell where the next push will come from, but he soon finds out that it will come from somewhere at every minute. He must watch the totality of Communist being always. This is of course a very tiring chore. The Communist power can rest when it wishes but its opponent can never rest at all. The outgoing zeal of Communism is endless and permanent.

As I have described it, Communism seems an unbeatable adversary. However, this is not necessarily the case. Communist theology may be a huge illusion. According to the theology of our own culture, it is an allusion, albeit a dangerous one. The leading theology of the West was once just as optimistic, absolutely sure that its way of life would inevitably prevail in all the world. It is more sober now and it recognizes that a utopian democracy may never be the universal human situation. We look at it as a consummation devoutly to be wished and a laudable goal for effort, but we now believe that it may well never come to pass. In our present theology nothing is necessary. Whatever comes about is necessarily there, but antecedently something else might have come forth just as well. The underlying energy-wind, which is the ultimate factor of reality, blows as it lists. Neither you nor I nor it knows whither it will eventually go. Evolution renders things more complex and that is inevitable, but it does not ensure one and only one form of complexity.

Now ultimate aimlessness is a hard future for men to accept, but the inevitable advent of a necessary configuration of contingent being is no easier to swallow. The Russian government may be very logical in its acceptance of Communist theology but it well may be that this theology is not thoroughly shared by the people under the dominion of the government. The government may be justified in its action by pointing to its faith, but if its faith is baseless, its action is rooted in unreality. The power it musters is in the people who possess it. As long as they are willing to give it to the government for direction, the government can do marvelous things, but the moment the power is contributed listlessly or not at all, the government, in spite of its animating theology, will collapse.

It would be unwise to think that the Russian or Chinese peoples have abandoned their newly achieved faith. It would also be unwise to think that, except for an ardent minority, this faith is universally orthodox or thoroughly vibrant. Older cultures carrying older and different faiths are still operative in Russian and Chinese life. Government cannot eliminate this influence altogether, even though it tries. In a sense, a people must adjust to its government if it wishes to survive, but by the same token the government must adjust to the people for its own survival. The theology of a concrete culture is in the people and not in books drawn up by logicians. In the forty years of Communist history in Russia we have witnessed many deviations from the pure Marxist blueprint. Some Marxist dogmas have been quietly dropped and others have been radically modified. Both Marx and Lenin proclaimed the withering away of the state and its apparatus. No such tendency has been revealed in Russian reality. If anything, the state and its bureaucracy get stronger as the years go by. The government simply cannot trust its own people. The faith of the government and the faith of the citizenry are not identical, though no one is allowed to formulate the faith actually in the human beings who make up Russia and China. But the heavy restrictive action of government shows that the faith of the people is not directed to all the goals of government.

In final terms Communism is as valid as its theology. If that theology is an illusion, finally Communism will disappear or undergo a sea change. Its value for the moment is its capacity to harness the power of vast peoples toward objectives unpleasant to men of the West. In terms of my own faith, it is a theological monster, but that does not prevent it from being an effective political force. An idolatrous faith can be a powerful factor in historical evolution.

My own preoccupation is the theology at work in our own country. As has already been stated, America's theology is double. Two entirely different theologies intermingle in our people. One has the advantage of being preferred, but the other stubbornly survives without being able to suffocate its neighbor. One is the faith of the literati and the other, oblivious of criticism, is at home in the hearts of a large sector of our population.

The reason why this produces preoccupation is that one and only one theology can produce one culture. If our culture is not unified, we are not unified. In the time in which we live, a people must be one in its aspirations and in its vision of the good life.

31

We have already considered naturalistic secularism, which is the privileged theology of our land. We pay lip service to religion and the churches, but actually our action as a nation rests on naturalistic secularism. No one has given us a systematic expression of this theory but elements of it are clear enough. It is an amalgam of skepticism, empiricism and pragmatism. It despairs of knowing reality in itself and restricts its knowledge to what is experienced. Experience is bedrock but it is reconstructed into symbols which are then used logically. It has its divinity which is the primary energy acting in the observer and in the observed phenomena. This naturalism will permit no appeal to anything not enmeshed in the order of the experimental. The ancient philosophical discussions concerning the nature of being are dismissed as fallacious questions. Being is either a logical term or a pointer to the data of experience. Naturalism can go no further. Substance, cause, essence and the like, are mere words with no objective reality except as terms in semantic discourse. There is here no room for God as the holy. He cannot be a point of reference. But unlike other naturalisms of the past, our naturalism has no quarrel with religion. With condescension it treats it as a sociological and psychological phenomenon. For naturalism there is no less truth in Hottentot worship than in Christian cult. Truth is irrelevant to both of them. Men show a propensity for the objectivization of the holy and this is the explanation of religious theology. Instead of erecting a rational morality in terms of usefulness for social coexistence, defective moralities are constructed and then justified by the mythical will of God. Man has no afterlife. Such a notion is the wishful expression of man's desire for a good life. His failure to produce it in the here and now has moved him to locate its realization in an unreal world on the other side of death. This consoles him for his frustrations and gives him courage to be. But in truth, divinity, the ultimate, is cosmic power; morality is wisely organized behavior; the other life is a myth-making to poetize the stark events of experience which should better be faced by taking them as they are, and be dealt with rationally in their factuality, which means in their empirically observed impact.

In the academy and on the stoa this vision of life and divinity is taught. Its prophets believe in it, and they proclaim it as the good news of salvation. The journals of thought accept it and give it first rights in their pages. Any other theology is given tolerance but not approval. It has a similarity to but not identity with Communism, which is only a differentiated species of it. This similarity is now discounted and disavowed, but in the past of thirty years ago, American naturalism looked with a kindly eye on Communism. Its scientific spirit recommended it to a vision that prided itself on its rigorous scientism. Today the dogmatism of Communism makes it repulsive to American positivists but the theology of Communism is not altogether undear to it. Quite rightly; it is generically the same.

The young person's hunger to be advanced and free of the taboos of the oppressive previous generation makes our youth listen gladly and eagerly to the new theology. However, as youth passes, acceptance of this theology is less than total. The only element that remains is skepticism for all theologies. Yet in the total community there is a large sector that will not be deeply influenced by the new theologians. Most of our people may not be able to accept the "old-time religion," but they do believe that some kind of religious theology is humanly more satisfactory than the theology of the naturalist. The American is profoundly interested in morality, the scheme of correct behavior. The past has imposed on him a high regard for truthfulness, neighborliness, personal dignity and self-reliance. The religions active in this country regard these virtues highly and this draws many men toward the churches. But the churches have in general shunned ontological theology until very recent years. They have been moralistic and their theology has been a moral theology. The result is that our churches still have influence in our country but it is hard to say how effective it is. The influence is great enough to make Washington, Hollywood and Wall Street very conscious of the churches, though not in the least interested in accepting their norms. Religious influence certainly is not strong enough to make the theology of the churches in any way normative for public action.

It is not my intention to make a plea for the theology of the churches. I doubt if a cross-section of religious theology in the country is any more life-giving than the theology of naturalistic secularism. The tragedy of the situation is that both of these theologies are guiding the destiny of the nation. Our people somehow wish to retain both theologies, no matter how much they be in inner conflict. Atom bombs are made in the light of naturalism and their use is then criticized in the light of religiously derived ethics. Everywhere schizophrenia shows up in our political and social life. The reason is that our young men do not see visions and our old men do not dream dreams.

One palpable derivative of this theological schizophrenia is the art we produce. Our literature shows us confused, perverted, disoriented men and women. The poet neither condemns nor praises them. He puts them on the stage or between the covers of a book and justifies his action to a moral people by saying that this is what he finds in our life. The high tragedy of the Greek poets or Shakespeare is not with us. In its place there are suffering, small sins and obnoxious virtues with no vestige of greatness in the agents. Men do not cause their own destiny, good or bad, by choice, but rather they are victims of constricting conditions over which they have no control. They do not take up arms against a sea of trouble but with a howling whine they drown—and the spectator does not regret it at all. In general, religious theology is ridiculed and yet respected. Secularist theology is sycophantly praised but not really embraced. There is no will to believe in spite of the fact that faith is in the air we breathe.

This situation cannot endure. This is life in a void, too vulgar to be tragic and too painful to be comic. Man drugs himself with narcotics: comfort, good food, much drink and profitless leisure. But the power of the drug is not permanent; man must have moments of wakefulness which seem only to drive him back to the narcotics. Yet life is certainly a nisus to creation. If the creative power is only directed to ever more comfortable material living, the creative drive will wither. In this the Communists are wiser than we. They are quite indifferent to the people's cry for comfort, and will supply only as much as they deem necessary to keep their citizens from losing faith. On the other hand they stimulate the young and the old, men and women, to produce and create. They turn their attention to the colossal and not to the trivial, to advance forward rather than to stand comfortably still. Whether they will be able to continue their tactic over the long haul is a question. But there is no doubt what they are trying to achieve in their guidance of men.

The Communist effort is not too relevant. Governmental prodding and governmental lures will not solve the problem of creativity or of the road to greatness. These have only one source which is a strong faith operating within a culture and in those who live by it. What we need is a great faith resting on a big theology.

It remains for us to take a look at the demands of such a theology. It would be too much to ask me to construct it. Let there be no false hopes or objections to temerity. I do not offer the blueprint of the society-saving theology which must fill the void we are in. But we can discern what kind of light it should offer. We can see some of the demands it will make. What far better men than I cannot do is to give it such a glorious luster that it will charm all those who see it. But before we worry about the missionary effort to make men accept it, let us try to glimpse vaguely a vision more nourishing than the rank weed that is being offered us as food for the spirit.

3. A SAVING FAITH

In the previous reflections on the status of faith in our time, we saw that not only was there a conflict between the faiths of the different components of our one world, but worse still, in every sector there was a double faith intermingled in men and institutions. We have two forms of naturalism: one in the Communist countries and another in the lands of democratic organization. In each sector this naturalism is dominant. Problems of great human concern are solved in the light of this philosophy, which is a theology as well. Yet flowing through this faith, there is a concomitant commitment to a religious absolute inherited from older cultures which were the framework of human action in times past. In the West this religious theology can generically be called Christian, in spite of the fact that there are so many differing forms of it.

The result is that our people are neither totally

naturalistic nor yet totally Christian. It is here that we find the heart of our confusion. The Bible speaks of Yahweh as being a jealous god. This attribute is not only proper to Yahweh; it is the mark of any high god. The God of Christianity and the divinity of naturalism are high gods. They are not subordinate deities in a crowded Olympus; they claim total power and insist that there be no gods beside them. Yet as in the days of Elijah, the people are trying to be loyal to both of them. In this attempt they lose the protection of both divinities who will not consider as theirs those who also worship in shrines other than their own. We believe in God and Mammon, in human autonomy and divine lordship, in New Testament ethics and Lucretian determinism. We are in opposition to Communist naturalism because we have diluted it with a supernaturalism militantly abandoned by the Marxist leaders.

Now the reflective democrat and his counterpart in Communist societies see that there is good in the opposite theologies. Modern democratic prophets have seen that the social dimension of man is highly important economically and socially. We have left behind us the liberalism of the Manchesterians of the last century. No people in the world now entrusts the economy to the exclusive responsibility of individuals. Economy is a matter of a whole society. It cannot be made a reserve of an individual who is incapable of feeling all the concerns of the total community. Democrats have therefore socialized under the influence of the Marxists.

Communists likewise see that certain democratic emphases are valid. They have long given up the idea that the family must be jettisoned in favor of a fuller collectivism. They now foster the family and protect it. Nor will they apply the old slogan that each must work according to his capacity and receive according to his need. They give to the individual according to his productivity. Among the Communists there is the recognition that individuals are not at all equal by innate endowment, and the freedom of the individual to develop his own talents is acknowledged. Superior minds are recognized as such and they are not forced to level themselves down to the plane of the average. Such abler men enjoy a modicum of freedom, still small but constantly growing.

There are wise men among us who tell us that the present conflict in the world is not caused by conflicting cultures and theologies. They tell us that the Russian drive to imperial dominion of the world is not produced by Communist philosophy and theology. They find the source of Russian expansion in a power-drive to conquest which was equally present in Tsarist days. The Communists have only given a new rationalization to this nisus in terms of Marxist theory. Now the heart of such teaching is that faith has ultimately nothing to do

41

with the organized action of groups. People act because of instinctive pushes that are purely willful and unrelated to vision. No matter how they theologize, the Russians for centuries have been power seekers.

It is important that we keep in mind the analysis made by these scholars. They have found something, but it may not be something very new. Man is supposed to be a rational animal according to Aristotle's philosophy. The doctrine does not seem too hard to accept, for man evidently reasons in the ordering of his affairs. The great error would be to think that man is *only* a rational animal. Reason does not give us goals for action, but only ways of organizing the means to achieve the goals. Intelligence is a moderator of man, but by no means the stimulant to action. The psychologists of the last hundred years have made it quite clear that the roots of action are found under the level of consciousness and intelligence, where we find a seething opaque quagmire of desire. The conscious man, in consequence, not only reasons but he also rationalizes, and it is difficult indeed to discern which he is doing in any given predicament. The deepest drives operating in man are not rational; they defy reason nor will they be dominated by it. This particular observation is not a monopoly of the psychologists. Ever since the days of St. Paul, and even long before, religious men saw that man was under the pressures of ineradicable compulsions. They gave the name of original sin to this phenomenon. They considered original sin to be all-pervading and ultimately responsible for the injustices so visible in human history.

Hence to say that it is a power-drive that makes the Russians seek for world empire is not a silly statement. But we must not make the search for power alone responsible for Russian action. We know that certain organisms thrive in certain environments much better than in others. The meeting of right environment and innate nisus of the organism is the explanation of growth and vitality. Marxist naturalism is an excellent culture in which the Russian drive to power can flourish. The theology which is thriving in the Russian sphere of action enhances the potentialities of the craving for domination. If the theology were different, it might well paralyze the impulse or force it to seek other forms of expression. In Freudian language, the drive could be sublimated.

New theologies are communicated by men we call seers and prophets. It is wonderful what such teachers can do to the world. A scanty Jewish group in the first half of the century which marks the beginning of the Christian era, because of a deep allegiance to the vision of one man, roved over the Mediterranean basin and beyond it in one long lifetime, spreading the words of the Gospel. The Roman authorities were not wrong when they wished to suppress this wild-fire movement. It finally transformed the classical world, though this was not at all the objective which the new preachers had in

43

mind. In days when travel was not as easy as it is now, the Christian evangelists forced themselves quickly into every area of the known world. It was not merely their energy which made people follow them. They had a vision of life and eternity which was highly attractive to the men and women of their time. They gave man hope and the courage to be fully himself. They made of life a high adventure well worth living. This vision eventually supplanted the blurry vision which was the framework of Graeco-Roman existence. A new faith produced a new culture, always the actual way a people looks at life and behavior.

Thus far we have seen two elements in a saving faith. First of all, it enriches life in the sense that it gives it highly attractive values so that life is worth living. Secondly, though it does not remove undesirable dark unconscious drives which surge up out of the opaque unconscious, it does offer the means of sublimating such drives. The positively good drives are not hampered, but the drives which produce suffering and evil in the individual and society are given a healthier form of self-expression and outlet. No faith or the culture it produces will ever bring utopia to our world. The best we can expect of them is the production of the indispensable possibilities of a satisfactory human existence. Earth by definition is not heaven, but there is no reason why it should be hell, whose essence is boundless energy always frustrated.

We can detect more factors which a saving faith can give to a man and to a people. The collapse of Christian belief as the pattern for Western society was rooted in Christendom's refusal to accept the discoveries of the renaissance of the fifteenth, sixteenth and seventeenth centuries. In those days the esthetic and philosophic achievements of the non-Christian Greeks were seen again and they were alluring to the European. The Christendom of that time was slow in giving these wonderful things a home in its own house. Although finally it did accept them, there was a long period of suspicion and hostility.

The most important contribution of those centuries was the construction of scientific method. The churches were most unsympathetic to the new learning. They fought it and tried to strangle it. Yet the new discovery was highly appealing to contemporary minds and this appeal caused such men to withdraw from the churches, which declared the new learning meretricious and wrong. There arose the notorious war between science and religion. In this war the spirit of science overcame the opposition of the church which latter was left disgraced. Its influence on public policy and public action was so reduced that it was no longer a dominant power. It was relegated to a mission of protest. It could no longer lead and so it reluctantly became his majesty's loyal opposition. It is true that within the last fifty years the churches have embraced science nor do they any

45

longer heap insult and abuse on it. They even flatter it. But it is too late. Science gave a new faith to the West, and although, as we have seen, this faith did not succeed in destroying the old faith, it certainly robbed it of its controlling power. The result is that the two intermingled faiths, neither strong enough to annihilate the other, inevitably hobble the men of our culture, because of their adherence to an inconsistent scheme of the real.

We all know that in this day the ancient quarrel of religion and science is over. Our scientists toy with the idea of finding the holy and the church folk use and applaud science, but no one has shown how the two visions can fuse into one world view. It is not without significance that Père Teilhard de Chardin, simultaneously a scientist and a believer in the supernatural, felt the problem and in prophetic spirit made an impressive attempt to make one vision for Christianity and science. Whether or not he succeeded in his endeavor is not so clear, but there certainly is the possibility that he will rouse others to apply themselves to the task. Teilhard is a very significant figure in our moment. When one reads his writings, there is a feeling of religion and of science which makes science dynamically religious and makes religion whole-heartedly scientific. If Teilhard is not the prophet who is to come, he may well be his precursor.

In contrast to Teilhard we have the effort of the

Communist savants who wish to end the current cultural schizophrenia by the suppression of the religious factor in our culture. They insist that the two can never be reconciled and that religion hampers science in its saving work for the world. They overwhelm religion with sneers, jeers and indignities. They will not crush it out with extreme violence because according to their theology, religion is inevitably doomed. Hence there is no need to dedicate energy to its suppression when such energy can be more usefully directed to more doubtful goals.

One wonders if the Communists are not pursuing the erroneous policy of the churches of the seventeenth century. They sought the suppression of science by using the power of faith operative in their faithful. We know the church failed and there is no evidence that the Russians will be more successful. Isolated voices like that of Boris Pasternak, who was a distinguished cultural figure of no antiparty leanings, already show that there is among the Russians a hunger for the holy which forty years of governmental hostility have not been able to stifle. If one so long favored by the powers that be could still look for a star leading to the cradle of the Prince of Peace, the religious quest is by no means dead in a land which has magnificently put its own stars into space. The attraction of the holy is not a product of former economic systems, which did indeed give it

47

local coloring, but is in the very structure of man. Idols must do for those who know not God, but the high god is what is being sought even in idolatry.

A third element in the saving faith men need is openness to all things good. A theology which excludes or is hostile to values, old or new, which render human life richer in potential and inspiration is not salvific. It will not be able to be the foundation of a culture that will expand man and his existence. The only negation we expect in a good theology is the negation of negation. Borrowing Nietzsche's wild saying, faith must be a yes-response to life and all that is in it. Nietzsche announced to his generation that God was dead. But Nietzsche did not kill God, he merely indicated that the religious theology of his time was no longer vital. A vital theology capable of supporting a satisfactory and creative culture will be open to embrace every form of human good. It seems that the limitations on man force him to construct limited theologies. This is not surprising. Divinity is without limits but theology is only a human grasp of divinity, and human theologies show all the short-comings of their authors. We must also bear this in mind: just as we have no right to expect a culture that will give us utopia, so we must expect no theology to be a vision of God exactly as he is in his vastness and human incomprehensibility.

Our reflections have led us to the third component of the faith we all seek. We can yet discern a fourth note in it. It is in Toynbee's notion of culture that we detect it. For Toynbee, as we have already seen, all new cultures are sparked by their own theological superiority over a culture still at hand. For the English historian the evolution of cultures is man's slow ascent to God. Dimly on the top of the mountain of time he stands, wrapped in a pillar of cloud by day and a pillar of fire by night. In the rifts of mist or flame he can be dimly glimpsed. He is there always, silent and serene, but we are restless and in motion. From a vantage point higher up on the mountain slope, we can see just a little more of him. Every culture that carries man higher is a culture that moves up the slope to a yet better vantage point to discern God more clearly.

Not every culture is constantly progressive. Many, having reached a plateau from which they cannot move up or down, remain stagnant. They have reached a crag that does not lead up the mountain but hangs over an abyss of nothingness. Such a culture is a human outward thrust that ultimately fails. In its attempt to move up, it only moves out. It ends in stagnation and sterility with no possible escape toward the mountaintop. It must die or at best survive as a fossil. Toynbee points to such fossil cultures still detectable in our day. Zarathustra's fire cult is such a culture, still with us but utterly lifeless and unproductive of higher achievement in men.

In Toynbee we are given an important hint. A culture that has been successful in raising human society has also given man a better God-vision than its predecessors. However, it is continuous with some culture that has passed away. All which was good in the past is retained in an organic fashion in the new, and to the past goods a new good is added which binds the achievements of yesterday into a living dynamic vision of today. A saving theology preserves the beneficial insights of a former time and pushes them into a yet fuller insight for the present. As Toynbee sees it, when a culture can no longer make this fusion, it is dying and it is itself preparing the advent of something better. The dying culture will survive until out of its own death pains a new prophet is born to lead the people nearer to the promised land.

This fanciful representation of the evolution of cultures is full of sagacity. This sagacity is heightened by a shrewd observation of the English scholar. Toward the end of its life, a culture tries to achieve new energies by borrowing from other theologies. This is a period of syncretism and that means mechanical mixing. Elements which are not proper to a living theology are simply borrowed from elsewhere and thrown into the jumble of existing faith. The new elements have not been assimilated organically and have only been thrust into the lacunae of the preexisting whole. They do not affect the cultural faith organically and they either drop out as a result of the life's mobility, or they do not significantly influence the action of the original organism, which

50

operates on its own principle and lacks the new accretions. Putting an iron band on the joint of two pieces of wood will still result in a wooden beam. It will never become a steel bar.

It is here that we must be cautious, as Toynbee himself does not seem to be. An intelligent man can see what is lacking in a tool and he can see where the missing things are to be found. He will be tempted to try to add the missing elements to his tool but all too frequently its structure will not admit of the addition. We all know the inadequacy of chains for winter driving. The chains give the tire new grip which it did not have before, but the chains wear out very fast, especially if some of the roads are clear while others are yet snow-covered. Chains were not a satisfactory solution for driving cars in winter. They were makeshifts and not the real answer. The inventors of snow tires saw this, and they moved in the right direction even if they did not reach their goal. The tire must have within itself the traction needed for successful movement on snow and ice.

The point of the parable is that we cannot improve our theologies by borrowing things from without the system. If the root thought of the system has not within its own vitality the power to bring forth the element needed, there is no stable way of getting the new thing into it. For us this means that we cannot take factors of Buddhism and Hinduism and add them to Christianity. Addition means syncretism and what results is not a new living thing but only a patched-up dying thing. The patch will not save it.

Here, I think, we have the fourth and fifth elements we need in our saving theology. It must not be satisfied by a search for the ground of being. This materialism and positivism do quite well. It must search for a ground of being which is holy. Man must be led to prayer and piety. He cannot be sufficiently excited if all he has found in the depths of reality is an unmoved mover. That is naturalistic divinity. He needs to be shown the living God, before whom he can bow down in reverence, awe, trust, repentence and love. Then man has something to live for.

The pointing out of this God is the work of theology. Of course we know that God is worshiped in the churches, but the action, to be meaningful, requires that there be someone who will explain what stands behind the temple veil. This is the theologian. A valid religion lacking good theologians will be of little avail to the world which cannot understand what the religion has to offer.

The fifth element of a saving theology is that it draws the goods it needs not from syncretism but from the fruitfulness of its own system. Just bringing the churches together and gluing one upon the other will not make one big church. It will merely be a manifestation that no church in the whole group is big enough to do its job. Adding together many inadequate instru-

ments will not give us instrumental adequacy. What we
need from time to time is a theologian who is also a
prophet and who sees a new form of theology, though
not necessarily a new church. The new theology mani-
fests the inner potentialities of his church or if not of his
church, at least of the revelation already proclaimed by
God. In the light of this theology we shake the vision of
the past and it takes on a new directive power and shape.
We move up the slope of the mountain of history and
get a better glimpse of God. In that light we can maneu-
ver better in the mist in which we dwell.

Five things then we can say about the theology
which can save us. First, it will enrich life by preserving
all the blessings already at hand and add to them by
opening up vistas not yet seen. Second, though it will
not be able to destroy the perversity always operative
in man, it will point to ways whereby perverse drives
can be sublimated. Third, it will be an open vision of
life and reality, capable of absorbing whatever is good
for man. Fourth, it will be a recognition of the holy in
divinity and it will be in constant growth, moving ever
unto new heights on the mountain in the search for the
Holy God. Nor will it try to simulate growth by mere
syncretistic borrowing. It will bring forth from within
its own vitality the goods which at any given moment
may be lacking to it. Fifth and last, we need a prophet.
Ordinary men, especially those of high intelligence, are
able to see defects in a theological system. They are able

to point out what is lacking. They are capable of attempts at syncretism, but they will not bring forth an organism. For this we need God-possessed spirits.

It is the last requirement of the new theology which gives us pause. It indicates an absolute limit to our own powers. God-possession is an act freely initiated by God himself. Man cannot force God to anything because man cannot cross the abyss of infinity which puts the Holy God out of his reach. But God can cross the abyss, for with God no word is impossible. The prophet we need and want must be raised up by God. We cannot produce him.

This seems a very pessimistic note on which to end our meditations on the faith we want. Perhaps it is not really pessimistic but only cautionary. The beginning of valid knowledge is the awareness of the limits of knowledge. The understanding of any reality means the awareness of the limits of the reality we are confronting.

The affirmation of the need of a prophet in our time to lead us to a better faith than those operating in our world is not merely wishful thinking or cowardly refusal to be self-reliant and active. It is the first recognition of limitation which alone can make our efforts valuable. Our powers are greater than we think but they are not boundless. There are things we cannot do. But we are yet enclosed in a boundless, kindly power which we in the West call God. The movement to greater power and ever greater power must be a movement to the Holy God. No other divinity can save us. But it is the Holy God who must come to us, so often in a burning bush. There he speaks, and speaking he enlightens. With this light as communicated to us by him who heard his word, our human family is guided up to better levels of existence and coexistence.

No matter what comes in our time, if the individual grasps the truth of this theology and makes his act of faith on it, he is already saved. Salvation for the many is a problematic enterprise but salvation for the individual in any circumstance of life and society is not impossible. Horace, thousands of years ago, said that the upright man will be erect even if overwhelmed by a fall of jarring atoms. He spoke more truly than he knew. This much the theologian who is not a prophet can tell our generation. The upright man will stand erect no matter what contingency befalls him. What makes him stand right will not be his superior virtue or his superior knowledge but his faith. In faith we can live an adequate life. Without it we are lost. Charity is greater than faith, but only faith makes charity possible.

II.

GOD:

DEAD

or ALIVE?

1. *The* OPINION *of the* CIVIC ORDER

Although Nietzsche gave us the news of the death of God, he certainly did not believe it himself. All his life he was obsessed with God, at times in anger, and at times in fear, and sometimes in love. Karl Marx also announced the death of God and his followers make this gospel one of the bases of their thought.

Marx is more important for us today than Nietzsche. The tormented creator of Zarathustra is a milestone in the history of philosophy but he does not exercise a significant influence on the thought and action of the current age. There is today no Nietzschean school of philosophy. But Marx lives. The godlessness of Marx was not the product of any anger in that thinker; merely of impatience. The god of Nietzsche really was God, personal power and the norm of truth. Marx's god was no person, but only a product of ideology, and all ideologies were webs of thought spun in order to justify class domination with no reference to reality or truth.

It is wise to remember that Marxists do not fight God. They ignore him. Neither Marx nor his followers spent any time on proving that God is not. For them the god-concept is simply irreconcilable with their view of the universe and a hindrance to effective human fellowship in production and evolution. In consequence the god-problem is not for them academic. In their philosophic discussions the notion of god cannot come up. Their philosophy starts calmly with the postulate that there is no god, and there can be no return to a question which is logically prior to that stand. To Marxists, such a return would be quite stultifying because it would be illogical for them, since it would be questioning their prime premise. Yet religion for Marxists is a serious question to the degree that it is still an existential fact in the world. It is not an intellectual problem but a social one. In terms of political administration they must discover the most prudent policy of dealing with a fossil phenomenon, still about, but which is senseless and a hindrance. We know the policy they have adopted. In the body politic they are willing to tolerate religion as long as it is under their control. They have found out that it is safer to grant it a meager existence in the open rather than suppress it totally. The danger in suppression would be that it would go underground with an independent vitality working at purposes counter to their own. Modern Communism, as atheistic as ever, is not clashing with religion head on. It wishes only to surround it with an environment lethal to its survival.

It has frequently been said in the recent past that Communism is itself a religion. It has been shrewdly pointed out that Communists have a Bible which is inerrant, ritualistic assemblies, shibboleths, icons which are placed in every plaza and at every crossroad, even shrines for the incorrupt bodies of their saints. Communists certainly have a hierarchy which assumes quasi-sacral authority; they have ecumenical and regional councils where orthodox doctrine as contained in the Marxist scriptures and in the Marxist tradition are normative for policy. They have their dogma which is much more than a detached doctrine about man and the real as offered by philosophers in general. A Communist must believe; he must make a whole-souled surrender of self to the truth and its cause. This looks very much like what Christians call faith.

Now all this is true but perhaps it is not true to call this religion. The Communist way of life certainly employs all the manifestations which have usually been considered religious proprieties. If we define religion as the complex of such human acts and attitudes, then obviously Communism will be a religion. However, as Sidney Hook pointed out in a different context, we have in this hypothesis converted nonreligious people to religion by means of definition.

God himself is not problematic. If he exists, there is obviously no problem. There will only be the human task of relating to him in a coherent and consistent fashion. If he does not exist, there is even less of a problem. In that case the attempt to relate to him is doomed to frustration because you cannot be related to nothing. The true problem, then, is not God. Either he is serenely what he is, or he isn't at all. The real problem is what should man do when confronted by the god-concept. The problem is in man—as always.

A human problem is generally a theme for human discussion. Because a discussion uses words, we are inevitably faced with semantic difficulties. Just what does the term "god" mean? It is wise to remember that we are discussing the term with no attempt to define god. I had a friend who always insisted that friendship was his god. What on earth could that assertion signify? I think that he was merely saying that he saw in friendship the supreme good of man. Now to this god he could not offer worship nor yet could he pray to it. Such a god could not be found outside the context of human relationships, nor could it be the creator of heaven and earth. This god was what is today referred to by that detestable word, value. For my friend, of all the values after which men run, the most satisfactory was friendship. Nor was my friend singular in so considering god;

deeper thinkers than he have shown themselves willing to understand godliness in the sense of the supreme human value.

Yet it seems to me that in the long philosophic tradition the term "god" has a different meaning. When the Greeks spoke of the divine, they were speaking of something ontological rather than of something subjectively satisfying to human desire, although divinity could do this objectively. If we read Aristotle we shall note that the divine was for him the quest for and the discovery of the absolute starting point in the universe of realities. He explicitly called this kind of study theological. It had no religious overtones because Aristotle's divinity did not create the world nor was he in the least bit concerned with it. Prayer to such a divinity was senseless because it could not even hear the prayer, and if it could, it would be helpless to do anything about it. For Aristotle religion was not a worship of divinity but only a set of social rites and customs based on the valid recognition that there was an absolute center of the cosmos. Divinity grounded the intelligibility of the world but it had no practical function in it.

Aristotle's divinity is the model of all the gods of the philosophers. It is not transcendent except in a comparative way. The philosopher's god has no face, is neither personal nor impersonal, only an absolutized reduction of the myriad-formed action of the totality of reality. It is the center of a system of coordination without which the one world would not be one—a possibility the mind of man finds intolerable.

Divinity can say much more than this, but in this minimal sense it is achieved by all men without exception. If by a theist we mean no more than a man who recognizes that the unity of the pluralistic world supposes an absolute locus of coordination, then there are no atheists. The Communists insist that they are atheists but they recognize that there is a creative force for evolution in the material setting which is reality's matrix. Matter moving inexorably toward more humanly satisfying patterns of action is the Marxian name for the philosopher's divinity. Anyone who penetrates his own thought to its bottom, sees that an absolute is supposed in all his thinking. This Kant saw and this is all that natural theology ever showed, be it the enterprise of Aristotle, of Thomas Aquinas or of Spinoza. The objection to natural theology cannot be that it is not valid thought but only that it is too obvious to be needed. As an analysis of human thinking it is unimpeachable.

However, the name of the faceless god of the philosopher should not be written with a capital G. The philosopher's god cannot give man a religion, though religion certainly recognizes the reality of a philosophic absolute. However, man either personifies it, or claims to have met it in personal encounter. The divinity of religion is the upper-case God; it is more than the philosopher's divine; it is the divine which is numinous.

64

The word "numinous" has its current meaning from the work of Rudolf Otto in his study of the holy. When the absolute is holy, then we have the God of religion. Divinity which is only absolute is not God; divinity which is numinous is God the Lord. The religious man considers the philosophic divinity as a dim, hazy outline of God, but insists that God is much more than such an outline. The nonreligious man rejects any filling in of the hazy sketch which he regards as the absolute boundary of his thought about the real. His basis of rejection is that there is no necessity in thought to accept the added elements of the believer's God. Faith retouches the negative with which natural intelligence was left after its exposure to the world. With the plea of integrity, the nonbelieving philosopher refuses to accept anything for which there is no evidence, and as the writer of the Epistle to the Hebrews says, faith grasps things which are not seen.

Let us stipulate here that when we use the term "God" in these studies, we mean the numinous divinity, the God of religion, and not merely the philosopher's absolute. As we have said, no man, Marxist, materialist, positivist included, denies the reality of the absolute. This fact does not make such a man religious, even though we can find in him phenomena which are specifically associated with religion. He can rightly call himself an atheist, because *ho theos* (God) is numinous while *to theion* (the divine) need not be so considered.

In the light of such reflections we can say that the philosopher's god is not dead. Nor has anyone announced his demise. It is the God of faith who is supposed to have faded away. Is there any truth in this assertion?

First of all, the God of faith, just because he is acknowledged in the act of faith which rests on no evidence, can neither be proved nor yet refuted. Proof and refutation both demand evidence. No one has therefore proved the nonexistence of the believer's God. What the Marxists engage in is not an essay in proof or disproof. They simply begin with a different act of faith according to which the reality of the revealed God is utterly irrelevant. Their concern is a satisfactory human society built by human hands, needing the undistracted secular effort of all citizens. God is only a distraction. He is therefore ruled out.

Have the non-Marxist societies imitated their foe? Many see signs to the contrary. Never before in the history of America have there been so many members registered on church rolls. The churches themselves are as busy as bees. They put advertising on the billboards; they use up much of the time available to radio and television; on the university campus where they were not welcome thirty years ago, they now bustle with every kind of activity. Few indeed are the newspapers which would dare to speak slightingly of religion. Even the old Atheists' League has found it expedient to change its name to the Tom Paine League. Hardly a voice is heard in opposition to faith. On the contrary, it is highly praised and widely recommended to the public. Nor is this phenomenon peculiar to America. It can be found as easily in the various countries of Europe, Latin America and the Orient. The Communists' anti-God program is obnoxious to most of the dwellers beyond the curtains—iron or bamboo.

All these things are indeed significant. But just what is their significance? Certainly all will admit that we are a far cry from the days when the will of the revealing God was considered normative for the heads of governments and for the framers of public policy. The separation of church and state, as friendly as it is, certainly frees the state from any obligation to follow the doctrines and laws of any individual church. We may say that in God we trust, yet no one understands that slogan as meaning that God we obey. We may say, "Thy will be done," but we mean only that we accept the inevitable consequences of historical processes.

Our governments operate without reference to the will of God. Most of them have no commitment to him in any way. The constitutions either make no mention of him, or where one or other constitution does make a pious reference to the Almighty, it is more in the fashion of ancient ritual than for any effective orientation. In fact, the slogan whereby religion should not meddle with politics has taken on the meaning that our political life is factually Godless. Yes, our elected governors begin their careers with an oath to God, but it is a solemnity which requires little faith and certainly no sharp awareness of the dynamic reality of the Judeo-Christian God. Rites of this kind, but omitting the name of the Lord, can be found in Communist lands as well.

It is true that in the majority of the earth's commonwealths religion is in no way harassed by government. On the contrary, as with us, it is actually favored. However, this does not mean that society as formally organized is religiously committed. We have found out through experience that such commitment would only produce friction for the community. God only causes trouble, and so with some degree of regret, we have prudently relegated him to the department of public rhetoric.

Perhaps the most interesting device whereby we deal with God can be found in the home of the United Nations. A meditation chapel has been built there. It is not meant to be the locus of public worship. It is more like an oratory; it is extremely small, and it was an afterthought on the part of the builders. On entering it, one encounters various psychological means of producing silence. There is dim light and symbolic decor, though no precise meaning can be attached to the symbols. There is no altar, but in the center of the little room there is a broad trunk of a tree with a lovely bowl set upon it. The whole intention behind this effort is to give those in the building an opportunity to commune internally with something or other. Certainly a Hindu can meditate here and find nothing offensive to his faith. This is true for the Jew or the Christian. A Communist certainly could find it a sheltered spot where he could think about life and reality in a mood not unlike prayer; prayer itself is not necessary. The central tree trunk can represent the absolute or the numinous, depending on the preferences of the spectator. It makes one think of the altar to the Unknown God which Paul found on the hill of the Areopagus in Athens.

It is not my intention to find fault with this little chapel. It is rather surprising that in spite of its ambiguity it is there at all. In no way is it the center of the building. It is more than probable that the majority of those who are working in U.N. offices have never entered the room. The little retreat is a gesture made not so much to God as to those people who feel that God has something to tell the United Nations.

This chapel somehow tells us what the political world thinks about God. The chapel is not an expression of the announcement that God is dead. It only states that the political powers of this world refuse to state whether he is dead or not. They are willing to cater to those who do not think that he is dead and they will cater to those who are certain that he is with us no more. The political man of our day refuses to take any stand on God. In his private life he may indeed do so, but

69

in his public life, never. The non-Communist politician, on pragmatic grounds operates on the principle that God is dead. The Communist accepts the same principle in terms of his dynamic ideology.

Neither kind of statesman believes that God is buried. Both know very well that there are many men and women who still cling to him. For the Communist this is exasperating and baneful, and he cannot understand why people do not know that God *is* dead. However, they have found it politically wise not to insist on a burial. They will tolerate those who still think of God, provided such men do not try to intrude God into the social, political and economic life of the community. God is relegated to the recesses of the individual's heart. He is not allowed to appear on the streets or in the factories.

The non-Communist statesmen are not committed to the stand that God is dead, even though they will not acknowledge that he is alive. The question of his life or death is the concern of the private citizen and the private societies he forms. All such citizens are very much alive and to that degree God lives. The concerns of these citizens are very relevant to non-Communist statesmen. Where they find a large body of citizens staunch affirmers of the living God, the statesmen will listen to them—but not to their God.

At the base of the body politic there is the social body which is bigger than the politically organized commonwealth. In that body God can be, and as a matter of fact is, very much alive. The two societies interpenetrate. For this reason outside of Marxist states God is clearly present, but I must repeat, he is not normative for the republic as such.

If my understanding of our present political situation in the world is correct, we are facing a paradox. In spite of the antagonism between Marxists and Democrats, there is agreement between the two that God must not have a place in the political life of a nation. In one case it is a matter of philosophic principle and in the other it is the pragmatic necessity of political action in a religiously pluralistic society. Likewise in the life of the two culture groups the living God of Abraham, Isaac and Jacob is still about. In a Red society he is hampered by every restriction possible to government and in the democratic collectivity he has the freedom of the city as long as he causes no disturbance.

It seems that our political societies in the world answer the question whether God is dead in the affirmative. Remember, the only meaning which the term, "the death of God," can have, is whether or not God is relevant. God is real or not, independently of government. But governments can and do take a stand on God, and both Marxist and Democratic governments treat him as dead. They need not revile him (as the democracies certainly do not do), but they do not consider him as Lord. However, God is always Lord. Our commonwealths are not only secular as they should be, but they tend to be secularistic, which they should not be.

Can anything be done about this situation? It is difficult to see how it can be ameliorated. We have discovered by bitter experience that any type of theocracy turns into an unbearable tyranny for many if not most of the dwellers in such a situation. Even in those lands where God dwells in the private lives of the citizens, God is not the same for all. One believer's God wants his faithful to abstain from work on Sunday, while another believer's God wants men to abstain from work on Saturday or Friday. One man's God permits divorce and another man's God condemns it altogether. If the republic tried to legislate all these differences, men could *not* live together. But we have to, for we are together.

It seems that ancient forms of political society are going through drastic changes. The cultural and religious homogeneity of peoples is melting away, and yet their political union is more imperative in our time than ever before. In the past the relationship of government and people was more personal precisely because the communities were spiritually more unified. The result has been that government is more and more depersonalized. It has become a machinelike device to preserve the conditions for living together. That a machine would have no answer to the question whether God be dead or no is hardly surprising. A computer answers no questions because it hasn't any. It organizes data fed to it, and the feeder may well have questions which can be answered for him by the correlated data.

Now the life of God is a human question. Under those circumstances it might be a little naïve to ask what a machine thinks about it. Hence it may be that it is not quite so significant that the American government or others like it, works on the basis of the irrelevance of God to its work. It is hardly more than we would expect from any machine. As long as the machine is not geared to strangle God, we need not complain about it.

From the point of view of politics, God might well be said to be dead, and yet he could be very much alive in the cultural unit which on the level of its political organization cannot deal with the question. Perhaps in our day the presence of God will not be felt in the words of a king or in the prescription of law, but that presence might be quite palpable in the devotion and piety of only one sector of the total community. This would be perfectly sufficient.

Looking back on the situation of the past, when the numinous was far more transparent to the man who was in direct and constant contact with nature and its forces, we find that the God-awareness was anything but universal. Studies made recently among the simpler cultures of Africa show that there is much deliberate

73

atheism in so-called primitives. Indeed they all practice magic, but magic is much more like infant science than it is like true religion. Likewise, the village atheist was a well known figure in nineteenth century America. Intellectual agnosticism toward God was a recognized feature of medieval thought. We call whole periods of history ages of faith, but one has only to read the preachers of those days to see that adherence to the Lord was not necessarily staunch.

We are inclined to foreshorten the past and give it a unity and a piety which were not necessarily visible to the actual dwellers of those times and places. It is for this reason that I am not too disturbed by the practical atheism of our governments. Some try to show that this phenomenon means that we are living in contradiction to our professions of religiosity. I do not think that this is the only possible interpretation of events. I do believe that the presence of God in modern society necessarily demands a modality which will be new. Shrines at the crossroads may mean that the community is aware of God, and they may also mean that the community romantically preserves anachronisms. I can readily believe that there is more God-presence in the iconless cell of a Carthusian monk than there is in a museum full of Renaissance portraits of fleshy Mary Magdalenes and naked Saints Sebastian.

An effective profession of faith by witnesses and

service on the part of a few convinced believers will make God more alive in a community than the mild and tepid agreement of a society that God's in his heaven and all's right with the world.

The life of God to the degree that the phrase has human significance says only that his reality can be seen in the creative faith of sectors of a collectivity. Governing systems in the past may well have been reflections of such faith on the part of the people. It was never the dynamic vision of all the people. Today our governments are structured in a totally different way. The famous phrase, "For God and King," was meaningful when there was a king. It would be silly for us to cry, "For God and the Department of Defense." When the king went, the couplet of God and king went too. But it does not mean that God went because the king went. The king's absence does not imply God's absence, but his presence in the modern world can no longer be associated with the impersonal government which took the king's place.

Hence in answer to our original question, from the standpoint of political life, is God dead or alive, I can only say that the witness of our political organizations implies the death of God. This political organization may be Marxian or non-Marxian, but the answer in both cases is the same. Though there seems to be no doubt about the answer, it yet appears that, given the form of modern government, its answer is irrelevant. It is the only answer it can give, not because the issue was studied, but because it could not be.

The question of the death of God in our day is one which must be answered by voices in our society other than those of government and politics.

2. *The* ANSWER *of the* INTELLECTUALS

Some years ago Julian Benda wrote a book which was called *The Treason of the Clerks*. In this title the word "clerk" was the unusual synonym for the intellectual. Actually the Middle Ages did not consider all clerics to be intellectuals. Those who were, had rather the name of scholastics, schoolmen. Back in the days of Socrates, they were called sophists and in irony Socrates defined them as men who preened themselves because they could teach young people how to make the worse appear to be the better reason. Plato preferred to consider the intellectuals as lovers of wisdom—philosophers.

In history they have had different names and were judged differently by different sectors of the community. However, whether considered highly or meanly, they were always around. In as far as there was a social

77

center for them, it was the institution called the academy or university. Not all were professors, but all were somehow attached to it. They were all contemplatives, not in terms of prayer, but certainly in terms of serious thought about things of the spirit. Scientists, philosophers, writers, dramatists, artists, theologians and professors in general are packaged together under the wrapper term, intellectuals.

Whether you like them or not, the intellectuals are influential in society. Sometimes they even have influence in government, but their record by and large has indicated that they are more often opponents to the governments of their moment. In any age they make their greatest impression on the student generation.

The human question about God is certainly the kind of query that men called spiritual and therefore it is precisely from the intellectuals that we could expect an answer to the question whether or not God be dead. Perhaps their answer is not worth much, but certainly it is part of their métier to give an answer to this question. This is especially true because they were the first to tell us in the nineteenth century that God was dead.

It is interesting to see a parallel to the Nietzschean cry in the ancient orgiastic mysteries. Devotees in their frenzy sang that Pan was dead. The paradox of the Greek act was that as long as there were plenty of men around to shout the death of Pan, Pan was very much alive. It was only when no one bothered to memorialize his passing that Pan was truly dead.

There is a difference, of course, between the cry of the devotees and the cry of Nietzsche. The German philosopher was not engaged in a ritual which was in itself religious. He was serious when he announced the death of God. Do modern intellectuals confirm the news given by their colleague to nineteenth century Germany?

It must be admitted that many philosophies current in our day are generally cold toward the Judeo-Christian God. Positivism, naturalism, existentialism, empiricism, pragmatism, materialism and scientism consider God, in the words of old Laplace, a hypothesis of which they have no need. It is not impossible for a young man or young woman of our time to go through four years of college, delving into science, philosophy, linguistics and history, either without ever hearing the word God at all, or, if God is mentioned, with the insinuation that he is dead.

It is also true that ours is not a sacral culture, but secular, though not always secularistic. We need only pick up our weekly reviews of events. There we find, somewhat in this sequence, national events of topical significance, international news, and then in no set order, the current activities in the fields of human concern: art, theater, medicine, science, athletics, religion, education and books. Religion is treated impartially from the viewpoint of the detached journalistic reporter of phenomena. The journal cannot in today's framework of mores support any one religious view, and the whole field of religion is treated as if it were quite homogeneous in substance and a partial concern among many others in the life of society.

Now this is a judgment on religion. The genuinely religious man does not believe that his religion is a subsidiary interest in his life. Religion directs and dominates all that he does. God for him is Lord, the norm of truth, the guide of life, the law for action. This religious attitude is not shared by our journals even when they are most friendly to the religious enterprise. Rather, religion is considered as one of many human activities and by no means the most important. This mode of presenting religious life is not an affirmation that God is dead, but it certainly implies that the old God who was creator and king of the universe is dead. A much smaller god has taken his place, a god who is by no means jealous and quite ready to share along with other interests the allegiance of men. The divinities of India and Africa, the God of Protestantism, of Catholicism, of Judaism, are democratically treated in the realm of divinity nor are they put over or under Allah of the Muslim. God is treated from the viewpoint of man's religions and these are all considered as homogeneous—even though they protest such a view.

In the not so distant past a man in difficulty because

of his failure to solve adequately the problems of behavior was sent to a clergyman. Here he was supposed
to find moral guidance and the motivation to carry it
out. Today this is not the first solution. We have experts trained in the behavioral sciences: psychology,
sociology and psychiatry. To these men we send our
victims of malaise. Such experts need not believe that
God is dead, but surely whether he be dead or alive,
they can in their work ignore the whole question. If
I go to a psychiatrist, my relevant preoccupation is
whether or not he knows his own craft. I can bracket
the question of his religious views. Human manifestations of what we formerly considered to be spiritual, all
but independent of the body, are today by common
consent put into a category parallel to those which the
physician and surgeon make their own.

The point I am trying to make is not that all these
developments are illegitimate or that they should be
dropped. I wish only to indicate that the intellectuals
who organize all these things have narrowed the field
of religious concern to a very restricted area in human
life. To make their whole effort more significant, the
little area which they do leave to religion by way of
condescension rather than respect, is labeled as outside the realm of intellect. In the religious area you can
indulge in the weirdest fantasies and the grossest follies
without any criticism. Religion has become the rumpus
room of the house we live in, segregated from the home

proper, and subject to none of the disciplines holding the rest of the abode in order. A man's religion is his personal concern. It is not a matter of collective significance, much less responsibility. A scientist of prestige can suddenly practice voodoo and his friends put it down to a personal quirk, but they will not discuss the matter with him. It is sacrally personal, and not subject to communal inspection.

The growing secularism of our culture, fomented by our intellectuals, in its own way reechoes the cry that God is dead. But once more we must avoid growing angry in panic. In puritanical New England there were witch-hunts. This to us is a sign of how benighted the Puritans were. However there is another element in the phenomenon which must not be overlooked. At least some of the witches thought they were such. Certainly some of them did celebrate witches' orgies. The total phenomenon was not merely the invention of malicious or ignorant observers. The Black Mass is an ancient superstition, but it could not exist except where the White Mass was a common occurrence. The medieval man with psychiatric troubles did go to the priest not only because the priest was a representative of God, but mainly because he was supposed to be wise in the ways of man as well. The priest was a self-trained psychiatrist, hardly scientific but at the same time not altogether superstitious.

At the University of Paris professors in the thirteenth century taught openly doctrines which are not unlike doctrines proposed today. Preachers and reformers like Savonarola thundered against the secular culture introduced by the Renaissance. They saw it as godless and anti-God. Much of it certainly was. The relaxed moral example of ancient Greece and Rome was being held up to the Christians of fifteenth and sixteenth centuries as a more adequate orientation for life, and the intellectuals who organized this campaign were quite successful. No age made God totally alive in its societies. Such is the story told by the Bible, and that book was written with every bias in favor of Yahweh, God.

In other words, we must not look at our secularism as something altogether peculiar to our age. It is concededly true that our intellectuals today need not concern themselves with the prestige of God as their predecessors in other times and places did. God today is certainly a more hidden God than he ever was before. He is not as visible to us in nature, in art, in thought, in customs as he was in certain periods of our past.

But let us not exaggerate. The California Forty-Niner, so famous in song and story, was not what we call a religious man. I know the story of a group of Canadian nuns who took the long trip from Montreal to San Francisco by way of Cape Horn. When they arrived at their destination, the bishop of San Francisco would not allow them to debark, for, as he told them, he could not protect them if they landed. They had to return to Chile to exercise the philanthropic energies which they had destined for California. The secularism of modern San Francisco may be no less than that of 1849 but certainly it is not worse.

There is another feature in the activity of our modern intellectuals which needs a little consideration. In this country one of the organs of the intellectuals of less conservative tendencies is the *Partisan Review*. It is not Red, although some panicky souls think so. It is just as truly not a religious journal nor do the majority of the contributors to the review accept any restrictions imposed by any orthodoxy other than that of liberalism. (Incidentally, the liberal's orthodoxy can be just as stuffy as any other -doxy.) In 1950 the review published a little symposium entitled: *Religion and the Intellectuals*. The contributors to the collection were all men and women whom the journal, a connoisseur in the matter, considered to be intellectuals. There were twenty-nine in all, including names like A. J. Ayer, John Dewey, Jacques Maritain, Sidney Hook, I. A. Richards and Paul Tillich. The book is thirteen years old but things have not changed substantially since that time.

What concerned the editors of the volume was the revitalization of religion in America. It was not so much that people at large entered into the religious revival, but much more, that in the ranks of the intellectuals religion was rising again. An observation from the preface of the book is highly significant, given the nature of the group publishing the symposium (p.5):

If we seek to relate our period to the recent past, the first decades of this century begin to look like decades of triumphant naturalism: and if the present tendency continues, the mid-century years may go down in history as the years of conversion and return. In this comparison we notice in particular that whereas for a long time modern thought envisaged a future society that could and would exist without religion, at present many thinkers sound an insistent note of warning that Western civilization cannot hope to survive without the re-animation of religious values.

Now what is simply taken for granted in the whole volume is that the intellectuals who only a few years ago were solid in their naturalism and in their rejection of the transcendental God of the Hebrew-Christian tradition, were now changing their minds. Sidney Hook in his essay (pp. 70–77), considers it all a failure of nerve which had already been a current by the end of the Second World War. However, he declares it to be a "tidal wave" in 1950. He himself did not lose his own faith in naturalism and he tried to explain why so many others did. His own faith being so strong, he could only courteously regret the desertion of former comrades and he could easily find what he considered fallacies involved in the new positions.

However, no matter how Sidney Hook understood the failure of nerve of the intellectuals, the fact remained that he could no longer consider himself the spokesman for all of them. Actually spokesmen of tendencies quite different from his reached the public ear more persuasively. In fact, Hook's explanation of the intellectuals' return to the God who had been somewhat prematurely declared dead, sounds dubious. For the New York philosopher, the conversion of the intellectuals was a matter of failure of nerve. Just why it requires more nerve to reject almost offhand the mysterious God of faith than to accept so frightening a belief is not clear. If the nerve involved was the one shown by the naturalist by breaking from the comfortable orthodoxy of the early part of the century, was there not the same amount of nerve shown fifty years later by those who left the comforts and security of liberal orthodoxy? If it takes nerve to stand one's own ground, refusing all foreign aids, real or assumed, does it take less nerve to give up that very real position in favor of one of no empirically tested security?

The really telling confirmation of the validity of Sidney Hook's evaluation of the trend among the intellectuals toward religion was his own review some years later of a volume done on Reinhold Niebuhr (*New York Times Book Review*, New York, Jan. 29, 1956, pp. 6, 7, 22). In it he complains that Niebuhr is at heart no less a naturalist than Hook himself, hence why should so much fuss be made about Niebuhr? The validity of Hook's criticism of Niebuhr need not be discussed here. Yet it is strange that Hook, who refuses to be made a convert by definition, makes Niebuhr a naturalist by the same tactic. But the important point is that Niebuhr in terms of religious concern seems to make more sense to many intellectuals of our day than Hook, whose own doctrine is proffered as scientific, liberal and genuinely orthodox by the standards of 1900.

In the symposium to which I have been referring, there is also an article by Paul Tillich, a theologian in close contact with current life. He says (pp. 136–137):

> The fact that there is a turn toward religion among intellectuals cannot be questioned. The literature of the last decades is a continuous witness to the fact. It is difficult to find in the outstanding recent philosophers, novelists, poets, playwrights, educators, psychologists, physicists, anybody who would stand for the shallow atheism or optimistic secularism of two or three generations ago. —This development is not a "failure of nerve" but it is the courage to see what a favorable historical constellation had covered for almost a century; what could not be hidden any longer, the dark underground of the personal and social life.

Now the reason why I have introduced this little book, *Religion and the Intellectuals*, is that it is a trustworthy witness to the fact that the circle of intellectuals, who told us sixty years ago that God was dead, is no longer the courageous prophetic band united in writing God's obituary. In fact it is no longer fashionable to exult in the old Tryant's death, for, behold, he is risen and is with us again. This is frankly stated by recognized members of the intellectual brotherhood. Not all intellectuals, not even most of them, are persuaded that God is no more.

Now far be it from me to say that the God who has come back is exactly the God who went into eclipse. In an environment where it is difficult for God to come back, in Communist Russia, a prophet did arise to tell us that he has discreetly returned even there. Boris Pasternak makes Doctor Zhivago his mouthpiece and the doctor professes faith in God, not merely in the Marxist philosopher's absolute. Nevertheless Doctor Zhivago's God is not the same one which the Russian Orthodox Church proclaimed and still proclaims. He is totally different from the Marxist principle of dynamic matter determining the evolution of history and he has more of the texture of the God preached under the onion domes of Eastern Orthodox temples. But he is a different God. The question now arises: is Orthodoxy orthodox?

Believers in God no doubt have reason for looking at the intellectuals with an emotion less than gratitude. That brotherhood spread wide the notice that God was dead. However, this was done in the bad old days. Today the same report is still given in the same circle by some of the initiates, but the voices can no longer be called representative, even though they are genuine enough. There are other voices like those of Toynbee, Malraux, Heidegger, Eliot, Greene, Aldous Huxley and Buber, unorthodox believers and yet genuine intellectuals all, who speak to our generation of the living God.

The problem I find in the intellectuals is not in their consent to the rumor that God is dead. They did not start this rumor. The liveliest of them deny it altogether. They feel that they have brought God back and they are the first to give testimony that he is not dead. Yet they may be doing him a disservice. I sometimes lean to the idea that they have made only a conditional surrender, and the conditions are somewhat unworthy of the Lord.

There is one thing that intellectuals prize very highly and they are very sensitive about it. It is what they call their integrity. The word in the abstract is a lovely profession of dedication to truth in its fullness and entirety. The intellectual's pursuit of such truth is certainly the hallmark of his guild. What would certainly turn their lives into misery would be the realization that they were frauds or hypocrites. The very heart of scholarship is to pursue truth as far as it can be achieved. The road may be long and tortuous, but the scholar, in terms of his dedication, will follow it wherever it goes. This is the nobility of the craft and the reason why society at large admires and reverences the guild.

Yet we know that the scholar is only a human being. The description of human action with which Freud enriched the world brings out quite clearly the fact that no mind is so free from the distorting tendencies of the *id* that it can mirror the truth just as it is. The mirror is bent and the reflections on it must appear somewhat twisted.

The intellectual's psyche is no different from that of the common man. What puts the curves in the intellectual's life is the upsurge of unconscious desire that is at work in human beings. Strange as it may seem, it is comforting to be supported by the ideas that are the common property of all about us. There is the type who must fight the common persuasion, because he feels a compulsion to overcome an all-too-easy tendency to accept every suggestion that is offered. The subject aware of this propensity overcompensates his inclination to gullibility by fighting against every condition imposed by his environment or suggestions proposed by anybody in it. Such a man is not defending his integrity but rather he is fighting to be himself under hostile conditions. But the conditions are in himself, not in the situation. At this moment we are not interested in such a person. We are thinking rather of the individual who is constantly scrupulous lest he betray the truth, so that his scrupulosity really becomes an obsession rather than

90

a valuable instrument in the understanding of reality.

The intellectual who is of this kind is not an ignoble knight, but he can be an enemy of truth because he will not accept her unless she permits him to approach her in doubt and marry her in possible infidelity. But there are intellectuals who are not fully noble, and at times and in some one place the whole guild of intellectuals falls into the category of the despicable. During the Hitler years in Germany the price for being an intellectual was that the thinker had to agree with Hitler's own world vision and in addition he had to be a herald of it to all men. Now Hitler's ideas, as the whole world today admits, and as many in those days clearly saw, were atrocious and without substance. Yet the German brotherhood of intellectuals did not raise its voice in protest. Many of course had to leave the country but those who remained, among them top-notch scholars, either said nothing or even lent themselves to Hitler's destructive notions. Some even began to peddle Hitler's wares.

Those of my generation who witnessed this degrading spectacle, even though they also work in the intellectual's field, will never forget. It makes these workers wary of the brotherhood, but the glory of the fraternity is hard to ignore. It can even strengthen his attachment to integrity, but an overcompensating attachment to integrity can be an obstacle to docility which is a necessary prerequisite to faith.

On top of this operational disease among the intellectuals, there is another element to bear in mind. The God of our fathers was a self-revealing God. He met man in faith and freedom. He could not be deduced from the principles men find operating in the work-a-day world of experience. The intellectual by his lofty code is constrained to search for truth according to the guiding threads he finds in man's general confrontation with the real. To the degree that he stays exaggeratedly faithful to such a manner of procedure, he excludes himself from the experience of an encounter, free and paradoxical, with the unique Lord. The intellectual is not the man best equipped to tell us much about God. The man who is humble, prayerful, docile and moral has a better chance of walking with God. We call him the saint; he may also be a scholar, but the scholar in general is something like the rich man who is far too bulky to pass through the eye of a needle.

Hence we must not expect too much from the intellectuals in our quest for God. Only three generations ago they told us God was dead. Today many of them laugh at their predecessors, and tell us that God is very much alive. On their own word, it is evident that the intellectuals were misleading guides in the past. There has been nothing so changed that the new members of the class have a higher degree of infallibility than their fathers had.

This comes to us clearly in what the intellectuals tell us about the supposedly dead God whom they have found to be really alive. The God they find is not exactly made in the image of the God of the perennial Hebrew-Christian tradition. That older God was he after whose image and likeness man was made. The rediscovered God seems something revised to correspond to the image and likeness of man. At times one wonders if the intellectuals of our moment do not simply take the philosopher's absolute and cover it with the robes of God. It is hard to see that the God so many of our modern prophets proclaim loves us or cares about us. For many he seems to be something away off in outer space so that we cannot see him at all and we must content ourselves in knowing that he is there, although we can never really know him as he is.

Others tell us disdainfully that the world is too small to hold the Lord. He does not enter into the murkiness and fogs of our little earth. We know that he is there by a strange sense of his presence exercised by the absurdity of our own experience. Such things I cannot understand. They give me a strange solace, for they tell me that it is impossible to understand, and that answer by itself does not irk me. Yet the intellectuals themselves seem to understand something that I do not and I would like to know how they achieve such understanding.

Perhaps I am too worried about the intellectuals. It would hardly be surprising if it were so, because with timidity and fear of being laughed at by them, I like to think that I belong to their congregation. Perhaps the wisest thing would be to fall back on what the believer knows, namely that the God of old could not be discovered by mere human wisdom, although true wisdom and the fruits thereof were his. In graciousness he came to the humble and repentant of heart, to the heart that was open and not closed. If this be the truth, then we find that the intellectual and his brotherhood are quite irrelevant in their answer to the question of God be living or dead. They are irrelevant when they say that God is dead and they are just as irrelevant when they tell us that he is alive. The current intellectual willingness to tell our generation that God is alive will make the believer's position in society easier. But ease of belief has never been a guarantee of its validity. In fact, that it is hard seems to be a bitter sign of its genuineness.

Once more we have come to the conclusion of the previous chapter. Though the God of faith is more congenial to our current intellectuals than to our political society, the validity of faith and the arduousness of its exercise are not in any way enhanced or modified. When the majority believes and speaks well of the God of faith, we may legitimately begin to fear. In the words of the supreme Master of Christianity, believers form his *little* flock. If they are a large herd, their shepherd may very well be some one other than the Lord.

3. *The* WITNESS *of the* CHURCHES

A completely detached critic would perhaps tell us that it would be senseless to ask the churches if God be dead. He would rightly point out that they are biased witnesses whose testimony could hardly be trustworthy. The churches in order to exist must believe that God did not die. Their own self-interest, be it noble or base, simply renders them incompetent to make any impartial declaration on the question which is the stimulus of these reflections.

However, biased though they be, we must ask them our question. They are the only specialists in our field of inquiry. They are the only ones who claim that they have been and are in rapport with the numinous God. The expert, even when biased, must be interrogated in matters belonging to his speciality. We shall keep in mind the churches' bias and try to perceive where their prejudgments could significantly affect their testimony. The admissions of the churches against their own interest would be telling evidence whereby we can come to a reasonable decision.

The churches certainly insist that God is alive. They are doing it today with impressive vigor. Churches on the free side of the Iron and Bamboo curtains are shouting it louder than ever before, making full use of all modern facilities for communication. Even behind the curtains the churches are by no means dead. There are churchmen who insist that it is precisely in those areas that we find the strongest believers. In such lands the man of faith must be ready to pay a high price for his religious commitment, ever so much higher than his brother who lives in lands which do not war on faith. Seemingly reliable statistics reveal that one-quarter of the Russian people still accept the doctrine of the Russian Orthodox Church. The seminaries still functioning with the permission of the Soviet government, something less than twelve, are crowded with students who are all young men for whom this choice of vocation is detrimental to their civic status. The probabilities are great that the three-quarters of the Russian people who today do not affiliate with the Russian Orthodox Church offer us a percentage which is exactly the same as it was in the days before religion was put into a straitjacket. In those days three-quarters of the population may well have belonged to the church only in the most nominal sense of the word. Today, with no advantage for even so thin an allegiance, they have dropped what never was very real.

Does the vigor of the churches mean very much? Perhaps not. Granted that in the past much religious adhesion was purely formal with little inner awareness, yet the thought pattern set for governors, publicists and leaders included the recognition of the relevance of God to public life. The churches today do not have the power to make our civic leaders take such a stand. The political heads of Germany, France and Italy seem to be men of religious conviction but their policies would be the same if they had no religion at all. In conversations with the Marxist statesmen, God does not even have the opportunity of being scoffed at. He has no part whatsoever in the discourse. In other words, the churches have lost their directional power in our world. They do not have the numerical strength to be any more than a minority, one not to be forgotten entirely but hardly of sufficient influence to make their own visions of life decisive for public policy and decision. The weakness of the churches is a witness that in the realm of national and international life God, if not dead, is certainly of no great consequence.

As we saw in an earlier chapter, this fact is not so telling as one might assume at first sight. In the secular order where the churches are so discordant in their testimony to God, secular authority has no other recourse than to evade the question altogether. This it can do and yet be blameless in its practical atheism, for secular living together and secular progress need authority even though no religious framework hedges them about.

It is the discord of the churches which must be considered. Because of it, the secular order is forced to keep God out of its affairs. Does the discord also say something about the living God? It has said and is saying much.

First of all, the God of most of the nineteenth century churches is either gone or so parochial in his existence that the general world is not aware of him. That God belonged to the literalistic interpreters of theological propositions. He was the God who made the whole universe in six days of twenty-four hours each. He was arbitrary and whimsical in his demands. He was utterly voluntaristic. It would not be fair to call him a Fundamentalist God, because many Fundamentalists did not nor do now so conceive him. Rather he was a God who looked too human. He was made to the image and likeness of the Victorian father. In the light of the witness of the churches, the Victorian God is dead. His passing has not been regretted.

But even in Victorian times, there were other gods. The God of Deism had not yet fully disappeared. He was the great unknown and the great unknowable. His function was to inculcate a morality of sobriety, industriousness and responsibility. He usually had an incidental chore; he was to keep people content in their appointed places in life. He favored the rich, for their riches were signs of his blessing given because of men's virtues. This God has also faded away and even the memory of him evokes the feeling of repugnance.

The god of the Victorians was not an eternal God. He was very much of the Victorian era. But in those days and before them, the eternal God was in the minds of many men. How has he fared? To answer that question we must give some kind of description so that we may recognize him.

The Protestant Reformation influenced the nineteenth century very strongly. The British Empire and the German Reich had their roots in Protestantism more than in any other religious vision. Britain ruled the waves and controlled Africa and the East. Germany excelled in philosophy and science, forming the thought patterns for Europe and America. World visions from India and China impinged but weakly on the nineteenth century mind. Hence it is that we must discover the eternal God as authentic Protestantism saw him.

In the sixteenth century Luther and Calvin did not envision God as any different from what he was in the ancient Christian tradition which preceded them. He was for the Protestant Reformers what he had been for Catholics and the Eastern Orthodox. He was triune, personal, creator of heaven and earth. One of the three persons, the Son, became man, taking his place in history for man's redemption in a way which left him truly God and truly man. Through the God-man, Jesus, called the Christ, a fellowship was inaugurated under the name of the Church which was to survive to the end of time.

If we stick to this brief and quite incomplete summary, we can say that the God of the Protestant Reformation was basically the identical God of Catholicism and Eastern Orthodoxy. He was the God of the West, but he was moving into new territory. The missionaries brought him to India, China and Africa. In those vast regions his presence was hardly impressive, but where the colonial powers were strong, he was becoming more respectable. He was standing up against the divinity inherent in Hindu thought and piety; he was a rival to the deity hidden in Buddhist wisdom. In Islam he made little or no impression, but all felt that the Moslem Allah and the Western Yahweh were really one. Both groups realized that the other group was of the same religion but heretical in its adhesion.

When Nietzsche announced in the nineteenth century that God was dead, he was thinking of the God of the Western churches. That anxious philosopher had a strong dislike for Jesus Christ, who in Nietzsche's mind had corrupted the strong manliness of the Germans. Nietzsche's atheism was totally different from that of his contemporaries, Feuerbach and Marx, both of whom were materialists. The visionary of the Superman was not preoccupied with scientific materialism; he was humanistic.

We have located the God Nietzsche had in mind. What is the witness of the Western churches to his survival? We must first of all say that the testimony is ambiguous. One voice which is widely heard in our day is that of the historian, Arnold Toynbee. He is a Christian and says so. However, he thinks that the Christian God is imperfect. This imperfection is manifest in the narrowness of Yahweh. He is a much too jealous God. If Yahweh would merge with the divinity underlying Buddhism, he would grow in stature and significance. If Jesus the Christ would only hold a place similar to that of Buddha and the other avatars, he would be a much more amiable figure. Toynbee certainly thinks that Yahweh-God is alive but he also thinks that he is in a stage of evolution to something bigger and better.

Now the whole supposition of Christianity was that Yahweh, made manifest in Christ Jesus, was definitive. We could not look elsewhere for divinity. For the moment, the question is not whether the Christians were right. Rather we must face frankly the blatant fact that Christianity in general up to the nineteenth century considered it specific to its faith that it knew God in an ultimate revelation which would not be surpassed. The revelation given finally and perfectly in Christ could permit, and in fact demanded, deepening of knowledge of its data. However, all the data were in the Christian tradition and more were not to be sought in any other source. In consequence, should any church make Toynbee's ideas its own, that church would be saying implicitly that Nietzsche was right. Such a church would be affirming that the God of its own tradition was dead. It would equally affirm that we look to the coming of a new God.

I know of no church which accepts Toynbee in his basic conception. In fact many churchmen have risen in protest against the English scholar's proposals. However, we find some fascinating positions uneasily tolerated in the churches themselves. Let us begin with a look at humanistic naturalism. It is not flourishing today but in the thirties and forties it had its American champions of whom Henry Wieman was probably the best known. For such theologians, all of whom wished to retain their adhesion to Christianity, God was not personal. He was instead the basic matrix of all human values. In a way man was dependent on such a God, but it was even truer to say that this God depended on man. God's reality was not denied, but all the attributes which the Christian tradition had attached to him were considered as untenable and outmoded. Once more we were told, and in the very study halls of the churches themselves, that the traditional God was dead.

We are decades removed from that moment and it is true to say that in today's theological classrooms the echoes still resounding from those distant days are faint indeed. Naturalism, historicism and revisionism have ceded to a new force working in our theologians. The new wind has many names. It can be called neo-orthodoxy, existentialist Christianity, biblical theology or theological revival. No name is exact and no theologian caught up in the new atmosphere wants to be labeled exclusively by any of these terms. Yet the new current has produced wonderful things. There is a genuine interest in liturgy as an expression of the Word of God. The Word of God is no longer identified exclusively with the written word of the Bible; the Word of God is salvation proclaimed in myriad ways. Above all, the Ecumenical Movement is stirring current theology in a vibrant way. Theology has ceased to be a mere study of ethical behavior as deducible from the Christian vision. In Karl Barth, Emil Brunner and Paul Tillich we see systematic theology thriving again.

All these phenomena are very vital and very significant. Have they anything to tell us about the life and death of the Christian God? They do, but the news is disquieting. We have seen that the God Nietzsche had in mind was personal, triune, creator, saviour and incarnate in Jesus Christ. Does the new theology think that he is with us still? Does it wholeheartedly ask: "Lord God of Hosts, be with us yet, lest we forget, lest we forget!"?

I think that many spokesmen of the Church give

us most uncertain testimony. When Rudolf Bultmann wishes to save the biblical kerygma by demythologizing it, is he protecting the New Testament or is he rather abandoning the Scriptures? His good intentions are beyond question, but is it valid to say that Holy Writ speaks only to the existentialist questions raised by anxious man? Even were it so, is this the abiding Christian understanding of itself and of its revelation? "Myth" as that word is understood today does not mean falsehood decked out as truth. It means rather the communication of truth in imaged language. This conquest of modern scholarship is of liberating significance, but it needs the recognition that myth is the inevitable vehicle for any truth that goes beyond the surface of experience. That the understanding of ancient forms of proclamation requires transmythologizing is a salutary insight. Images, which in certain times and places convey truth, do not necessarily have this power in contexts different from their original milieu. One image must be substituted by a more effective one in another time and in another place. However, the truth originally conveyed will remain the same, even though its concomitant imagery undergoes a change. Transmythologizing is always necessary, but demythologizing seems to be a break with the revelation as it has been handed down from generation to generation. If demythologization is the accepted task of the churches today, then the churches would be telling us that Nietzsche's God, the

God of the Christian tradition, is dead. In defense of the churches, we must gratefully admit that they are dubious about Bultmann's vision of the ancient God. But what frightens me is the fact that so many churchmen are only in doubt. "If the trumpet-call is not clear, who will prepare for battle?" (N.E.B., I Cor. 14:8)

Parallel to Bultmann's ideas we hear today a pained criticism of Greek concepts as expressions of the Christian kerygma. A seemingly healthy demand is made that we use biblical categories exclusively. If this exhortation were universally heeded, traditional Christian words would fall by the wayside. Trinity, consubstantiality, incarnation, hypostasis, and the word theology itself, are all Greek in their origin and not to be found in the Scriptures. Yet these words are rather important in the Christian tradition. Here we have a rather good instance of transmythologization and St. Athanasius recognized it as such. He met the objections of the Arians who pointed out that *homoousion* was not to be found in the Bible. Athanasius admitted its postbiblical character was obvious but he made the valid observation that the Greek philosophic categories as rehammered on the anvil of Christian theology expressed with greater adequacy the burden of the Scriptures. Not for one minute would he concede that the doctrine of orthodoxy was novel, but he willingly admitted that the imprecise words of the Hebrew writers were given a more pointed formulation for the Greek-thinking Church.

The current distrust of Greek or medieval categories is not because they are Greek or medieval. The words are suspicious to some of our religious thinkers because the words point to a metaphysics. The supposition here is double. First of all, metaphysics is considered to be alien and even hostile to the Christian revelation. Secondly, Hebrew speech was nonmetaphysical and, as such, is a purer medium whereby the revelation could be delivered to the saints.

Both suppositions are false. As Kant said in his introduction to the second edition of his *Critique of Pure Reason,* no matter how much you inveigh against metaphysics it will always be with us. Metaphysics is only the discovery of the assumptions behind any kind of thinking, and assumption-free thinking is as possible as a bottomless vessel. Christianity and its doctrine about God contain their own metaphysics and could not possibly dispense with it. To express this phase of Christian thought needs metaphysical terms, nor should it be surprising that the theologians will find such terms in the writings of philosophers of their own culture. Christianity has been with us for a long time and it has lived in many places. It is to be expected that in the evolving Christian idiom of two thousand years, Christian theologians found words of their time and place to be very suitable to express the message they found in the Christian sources. Such new expression, such glorious transmythologization, was not perversion or treason; it was the service of Christian thought to the Christian gospel. At any age such transposition is not only licit, but necessary. If the gospel is to be preached to every creature, the gospel must be expressed in the media of the creatures to be evangelized. That was true in the past and it is true in the present. There is no sin in introducing new concepts and new orientations into the perennial proclamation. Only one limit must be respected. The new forms must be filled with the same old doctrine. If the new forms make new doctrines, then they are not the communication of the message once and for all delivered to the saints, but rather the delivery of an entirely new gospel under the guise of misused Christian terms.

Nor is it valid to say that the Hebrew writers were free of metaphysics. What was typical of their proposals of ontological theses was the Hebrew incongeniality for precise logical categories. When they did metaphysics, they suggested it with image and symbol. They did not affirm it in logical terms. This may be a fascinating manner of doing metaphysical inquiry and it certainly has its own advantages, but it also runs into the danger of making nonunderstanding or misunderstanding probable.

At the heart of modern hostility to Greek categories for the expression of Christian thought, lies the refusal to admit that Christian doctrine is a thought-system. There is an uncriticized tendency to reduce the Christian message to an emotional exhortation toward any virtue dear to the exhorter. The Christian revelation, valid or invalid as ever you want to conceive it, is more than an excitation of emotion. It is also an appeal to intelligence in its own proper search for the real. Many of our modern theologians do not care for such a notion. They want to eliminate all truth assertions from the kerygma, or at least they want truth to be achieved in some way other than by intelligence. If they can push this conception of the gospel on the churches, it means that God is dead. A new god may be aborning, but the God of two thousand years of the Christian continuum will have died.

There is a third movement detectable in current interpretations of the Christian revelation about God. It has been called by some critics the revival of gnosticism. The allusion is of course to the groups within the Christian communities of the first two centuries. They were called gnostics because they made of Christianity a superior vision of truth, a deep knowledge which only the adepts could reach. The gnostics of antiquity were nourished on mystical ideas which were found in Persia and the East but had followers in Jewish circles of the time. The main emphasis of this kind of thought was that the historical accounts of Christian origins must be freed of anything truly historical. The traditional formulas must be understood as nonhistorical symbols of a mysticophilosophical scheme of the universe. According to their tenets, Jesus Christ was indeed the divine Logos but he was not to be identified with Jesus of Nazareth. The Logos was a divine principle at work in the world and took the occasion of the life and death of Jesus to illuminate mankind. Yahweh was not the true God; he was far too savage for the gnostics. The gnostic god was an ethereal reality which could be met only in mystical contemplation. The biblical descriptions of God and his Christ had to be so understood that they merely affirmed the reality of the High God and of the Logos which emanated from him. When we read the descriptions of and observations on gnosticism in the writings of a man like Irenaeus, we become quite confused. Irenaeus' lack of clarity may not have been the principal source of the confusion. The probability is high that gnostic teaching was genuinely vague and obscure. One thing which must be said about the ancient heresy is that it was warmly proposed and had a strong attraction for many men and, above all, women of those days.

I think that we can speak of a modern gnosticism. Once more we find thinkers who sincerely wish to be Christians and wish to advance the Christian cause. They may have been disillusioned with the literalistic presentation of the Christian proclamation of their youth. They may also have been deeply impressed by the obvious grandeur and sweep of modern cosmological visions. Certainly modern cosmology and moribund fundamentalism cannot be reconciled. They are two utterly other images of the world, of time, and of man. In such men the affection for Christianity was not lost, but it had to be understood in a way which would not conflict with the thought of our age. To achieve this end, they gnosticize. The Christian revelation contains for them no information about the events of human history, about cosmic reality or about God's own being. It only tells man how man should act in order to overcome his frustrations. This message is not reduced to mere ethics, for it contains basic orientations of a general kind. The Christian God, in his revelatory encounter with man, did not manifest what he was; he only taught man what man was. God spoke nothing of man's background nor did he promise a life in the world to come. In fact, he said nothing about any world, past, present or future. Incarnation is not something which encompassed God but only something which happened to man in order to teach him how to be godly. This ethical guidance was not given in terms of articles of law but rather as a broad principle whose applications could never be uniform in the endless variety of human circumstances.

Now the charm of this type of theologizing lies in its careful and sincere use of all the pronouncements of the Christian Church from the day she wrote the little books called the New Testament through the ages of the great Christian thinkers like Athanasius, Basil, Augustine, Leo, Thomas and Luther. Nothing consecrated by millennial tradition is denied or rejected. But it is all changed. It is not a mere question of transposition from one set of categories to another, which, as we have seen, is perfectly legitimate. It is in all truth the sucking out of the Christian message everything it meant to say by manifest intent and pumping into the empty shell of its rhetoric an utterly different content. Where this process is achieved, we are being told forcefully and without compunction that Nietzsche was right. The Christian God whom Zarathustra knew and whom the Christians adored was dead.

However, in Nietzsche's fervent poetry there was a holy man, who had not heard the news of God's death. There are men and women today who live their faith and hear the kerygma in churches, Catholic, Protestant and Orthodox, where they hear nothing of a dead God, where the whole emphasis is that their God is a living God. Him they adore nor will they bow the knee to Moloch and his thousand peers. It is hard to number such men and women. Nor is their exact number important. As long as they are here and form a cloud of witness no bigger than a man's hand, the God of the Christians is not dead. He may be irrelevant to the world at large and so be declared dead, but his Son was little concerned with such a contingency. His preoccupation with the world was not intense, nor would he even pray for the world.

We have reached a paradoxical and unpleasant

conclusion. We saw that the political order in innocent and indeliberate atheism acts as if God were dead, but refuses to discuss the fact itself. The intellectuals no longer shout the news of the death of God, and many feel certain that he did not die at all. It is in the churches that we find voices which implicitly though regretfully affirm the end of the Christian God. It would be impossible for them to say so explicitly but their inner conviction is clear. They are looking for a new God to put into the world. The old one is here no more. We hardly expect this voice in the churches but there it is. This is not by any means the voice of the Christian consensus either with the past or in the present. The message of the churches in general is still that the Lord God liveth forever and blessed be his name.

The upshot of our meditations is that today we can expect no earthly triumph of King Yahweh. Many who once said they follow him, walk after him no more. However, we must not feel disturbed for him. If tears must be shed, it must be for us and for our children. God does not die, but a world which thinks him dead, in all probability is on the road to its own grave. History teaches us that no nation was ever better than its own gods. If the God of our fathers is dead, then we can hardly be better off ourselves. This is a rather terrifying thought on which to conclude, but I can find no other.

III.

CURRENT

CULTURE

and RELIGIOUS

EDUCATION

IN an earlier part of this book we pointed out that our community, and all others, for that matter, in practice put the secular above the sacral in their collective concerns. Further, we saw that the Communist countries go beyond this preference of the secular dimension of life. They are antireligious, not only in practice but in theory, and they do what is socially possible to suppress religion altogether. Thus we concluded that in our time all commonwealths are secularist. One form of secularism is hostile to religion; the other is benevolent.

In the lands of Communist cultures religious education is as limited as is possible, given the religious temper of a concrete people. In lands where democracy is affirmed, religious instruction is unhampered. It is even fostered. In all such lands religious citizens are allowed to erect their own institutions of general instruction in which religion itself is a course of study. In some countries such schools are incorporated into the public system of education, for example, Scotland and Germany; in others religion is a prescribed subject for all public schools, as in Italy and Latin America. In our own country, the public schools do not include religion in their curriculum but they are not antireligious and in some places they offer facilities for religious education which, however, are not under the administration or responsibility of the public schools themselves.

It is imperative to see how American secularism operates. It has no intention of antagonizing the religious sensibilities of its citizens. It protects the subsidiary religious societies of the community. It recognizes that from a secular point of view religion is a good thing. Recognition of the sacral nature of reality on the part of a vast sector of the people facilitates the work of the lawmaker and police force. Virtuous people may be pleasant but, even so, they need at least minimal external law enforcement. Religion also brings forth a mystique which is an effective dynamism in national life. American secularism has, therefore, harnessed religion to its plow. As a national vision it is not committed to the religious, but it is anxious to derive all the good it can from the religious forces within the culture as long as they do not threaten to deprive the dominant secularism of its sovereignty.

In such an environment the religions of America exist and actually thrive. Within their own fellowships they have the task of instructing their adherents in the speculative and practical truths of their respective faiths. Now education is, of course, more than instruction. Education is a developmental influence on a human being. It brings to full evolution the innate potentialities of a man. In any society education is selective of the potentialities to be actualized in accord with the goods which the concrete society holds dear. In ancient Sparta the capacity for martial functioning was far more developed than in Athens. Spartan society was not prone to produce philosophers because this potentiality in the citizen, young or old, was not held in high regard. Speaking absolutely, a philosopher could come forth in Sparta, but practically it was difficult. The result was that Sparta made no contribution to the evolution of philosophic studies, although on the other hand, it did bring forth soldiers. In Israel there was a religious taboo against representational art with the consequence that Hebrew culture was incapable of producing great painters and sculptors.

Where cultures are simple, no systematic course of instruction need be constructed for the education of the fledgling citizens. They learn what needs to be known merely by living according to the customs of the community. The poets literally speak to all the people, and they explain the faith, history and values of the group. The artisans teach their crafts to their apprentices through doing. The religious and patriotic rites of the people inculcate basic ideas without recourse to logical discourse. Communal religion and entertainment, universally accepted customs and rituals, educate the growing person. We have in such a situation much education with very little formal instruction.

Where a culture is complex and the society is divided into distinct subsidiary groups, all with important functions in the whole, education must work out a system of instruction for the generic and specific action of the citizens. In a country like ours it is simply essential that all citizens know how to read and write because most of our collaboration depends on reading and writing. Our commerce and production demand a minimum knowledge of mathematics and this branch of knowledge must be taught. The child and adolescent cannot hear history and poetry around a campfire. They must be given it elsewhere. A community like ours is not religiously specified and general living together will not teach its children any specific religion. Hence the individual religions must instruct their young adherents.

Thus a complex culture brings forth systems of formal instruction. It is a fact that in this age political society has organized and maintains such systems out of the public funds for the benefit of all young citizens, theoretically without discrimination. For certain levels of such instruction the law imposes obligation on youngsters who are not legally free to absent themselves from schools.

In this situation the churches find themselves in a peculiar position. In simpler civilizations religious doctrine was taught by the whole of society. No subsidiary group was needed for the task. By living with the total group and partaking of its life, religious beliefs were absorbed just as the common tongue was. Religion colored all that was done by the community. Public worship, common knowledge of the Bible, family piety manifested in grace before meals and in hymn singing, constant and spontaneous allusions to religious life and doctrine seeped into the mind of every youth growing up in such a community. But this is so no longer. No local civic community is religiously homogeneous; certainly not in urban areas and very rarely in the country. Religious pluralism is the American fact. From the living together of such religiously plural groups no specific religious vision can be imbibed. Yet the churches need the young folk for their survival and, from their own viewpoint, for the salvation of the youth. What are they to do?

We know a number of answers given to the question. The first is taken from the action of the past when religion was taught to children and adolescents in the home. This solution no longer seems viable in our time. It was never true that the family was the teacher of religion in any primary sense. The home could and did focus the religious faith of the community or of a large group organized within it. A single family, with time, lost its own peculiar religious vision when it lived in constant intimate contact with a larger community which did not share the family's faith. There were indeed some stubborn folk who could keep their family true to the church of their fathers even though the general community had other beliefs. Yet they were few and they rarely could survive in their religious isolation for more than two generations.

Today, the modern home is not the institution

it was a hundred years ago. Home life is not as closely knit as it was in the past nor is there now so strong a family solidarity as in the past. Religion itself is now more extramural than in years gone by. Above all, the average parent does not consider himself equipped to give religious instruction except in the most general and insufficient terms. He wants the help of a specialist in this field as well as in all others. Even if he is equipped, when will he find time to give the teaching? He has his duties in the home and beyond. The young people are out of the house almost as much as in it. The time when the whole family is together is short nor is the mood of that hour favorable to instruction. To ask modern parents to give all the religious instruction needed by sons and daughters is an impossible demand and quite unrealistic. Parents can confirm and enhance religious instruction obtained by their children outside the home but they cannot deliver it adequately themselves. If the churches today must rely wholly or even principally on the instruction given by the parents, the churches will have no future. The home environment can educate religiously but sufficient religious instruction cannot be given within it.

There is another answer to the question of religious instruction which is widely advocated. With a good religious environment in the home, the churches can give the necessary instruction outside of the organized system of public schooling. In the abstract this solution is certainly attractive. The problems appear when one thinks of the applications of the solution. If what is meant is the system of Sunday schools, well known in our land, one can only shudder. Of course a Sunday school can be conceived which would be at least a partial solution. Good teachers with a well conceived program could do something valuable. Yet it is not rash to say that the majority of volunteer Sunday school teachers are distinguished neither for pedagogic talent nor for solid learning. The experience of so many children, and especially adolescents, is that the Sunday school is a bore and a waste of time. This is, of course, a contingent reality. The churches could and should recruit adequate teachers. They should and can construct effective programs of instruction. Yet even in the hypothesis of excellent Sunday schools, there are still grave problems. Sunday schools will give at most thirty-two hours a year to the pupil. A week goes by before the next class is in session. I doubt very much if parents would be satisfied if arithmetic were taught in this fashion. The child may like Sunday school but he will never consider the class as important as his schoolwork. Sunday is a holiday for the youngster, much more than a holy day, and class on a holiday strikes the youngster as a violation of his rights. Teachers in consequence make every effort to make the class entertaining, even at the expense of the solidity of the instruction. Anything like sanction for absence is really out of the question, and there can be little serious demand for homework. I am tempted to say that Sunday school is better than no religious instruction at all, but I do not have the courage to say even this much, because in the practical order many a growing boy got sick of religion because of Sunday school.

But as has been correctly pointed out, we must not consider Sunday school as the only medium available to the churches for religious instruction. We see all over the country religious vacation schools which are well attended. Then too, Jewish communities offer courses which meet at least five days a week after public school hours. In these classes the Hebrew language and Jewish religion are taught, and quite successfully.

Certainly these expedients are not to be despised. They have virtue in them. But are they adequate? As a matter of fact, are not the vacation schools largely attended by small children? Does the high school boy or girl go to them? Probably not. Yet it is certainly at the high school age that more detailed instruction is needed in matters of religious doctrine and practice. This is all the more true if little instruction has been received in earlier years. The good done in the vacation schools is real but it is not great, and for some mothers the reason why the child is sent to such a school is not exclusively religious. The mother has a splendid baby-sitting device to relieve her of the trials of children loose about the house and neighborhood, and it is cheaper by far to send her offspring to the local church than to a summer camp.

The yeshivas of the Jewish congregations seem to be nearer to the solution of the problem. Their courses are serious and the whole atmosphere is academic. Yet what percentage of Jewish youth attends such schools? I do not know, but I suspect that not even 5 percent of Jewish children are reached by this device. With my knowledge of Catholic children and adolescents, I can only say that there would be such resistance on the part of the young people in general that with us it would be an utter failure. To have spent a whole day at school as a prelude to a serious session of further instruction strikes the average Catholic child as utterly unfair. I am inclined to agree with this point of view. It seems quite unfeeling to make such demands on the majority of young people, even though it may be congenial enough for a few. As a boy, I certainly would have resented it to the point of rebellion.

All these solutions seem to me to be inadequate. If nothing other than this can be done, then by all means let us do at least this. Half a loaf is better than no bread at all. However, let us investigate the possibilities of something better.

We know that in some states the public schools give *released time* from their programs so that the pupils may receive religious instruction in their own churches. We know too that some citizens object to this arrangement. The Supreme Court has not yet unequivocally stated the legality of the device, though its approval seems to be probable. However, the hour given is an hour of the public school. This gives it a certain attraction to the pupil. He is using school time and not his own. Even if he were not to go to religious instruction, he would still be in school. From the stance of the churches the scheme has advantages. The boy or girl is personally involved with his church as part of his general school program. He has personal contact with his own congregation as a function of his student life.

The weakness of the arrangement is identical with the weakness of the Sunday school. Only thirty-two hours a year are given to religious instruction and successive classes are separated by seven days. Likewise the church can only expect the attendance of the pupil. No real sanction can be exercised on him for work done in the church school. Once more we are faced with a stop-gap, not an adequate solution. The young person majoring in classical languages in high school will probably receive more instruction concerning Roman and Greek religions that he does about his own professed faith. Yet *released time* is a better solution than Sunday school alone. The adolescent will certainly go to class and it is then up to the churches to provide good teaching in their own enterprise.

In addition to *released time*, experiments are being made with *shared time*. In this essay the public school shares its hours with a religious school. The religious school gives instruction in religion and in those branches vitally connected with it. All other subjects are taught in the public school. This arrangement avoids most of the difficulties we have seen in other solutions. The pupil is a registered student of the public school, though he is taught some of his subjects outside its precincts. The public school abdicates the right to form its charges in their totality and limits itself to a partial formation. This is really no great sacrifice because the public school, except in a totalitarian state, makes no pretense at shaping the total individual.

However, this solution is only in an experimental stage and it will surely meet with opposition from certain members of the civic community. Many educators unconsciously adhere to the theory that the public school should be the only formative influence in the development of the young individual. The mere existence of a coinfluence irritates them, especially if the other influence be religion in general or some religion in particular.

It is not that such people would subscribe explicitly to the principle of the monopoly of the public school in education. They grant the parental right to put the child into the kind of school the parents want, but they will offer no assistance to the parent in any way. If the parents want something different for their children, let them take care of it. The public schools are available and if they do not meet with the parents' desires, then the parents are acting arbitrarily and must face the economic consequences. Such people are hardly aware that they have taken a stand on religion. They want and do construct secularistic school systems. They will not allow the public to support any other kind. The result is that secularism is privileged in the community and religion hampered, though the general community does not profess secularism nor does it wish to curtail religious liberty. Allegiance to a secularistic institution becomes the mark of patriotism and adherence to a religious school a sign of un-Americanism. With no support in any constitutional declaration or in the actual ethos of our people, secularism is declared to be the force in which we trust. Where this idea prevails, the integrally religious man is at best a tolerated citizen.

To the religious man the religious training of his children is a necessary corollary to his own faith. For the religious parent religious training is the first necessity in the education of the young. Such a father wants religion to permeate the total instruction received by his child. Yet he can achieve his goal only within the limits of human possibility, and these limits are always narrower than we would like. The religiously committed parent must work out the education of his children in a concrete locus. The pluralism which is the central fact of American living together will not permit the permeation of all instruction with the spirit of one church's vision. This is clear and beyond dispute. It is equally clear that it is administratively and economically impossible to give to every one of the numerous religious groups a school to its liking. Yet such a liking must be a concern to a civic community which does not profess secularism as an ideology but only as a pragmatic form of coexistence. The desire of a minority must not be ignored because many difficulties are entailed in the effort to satisfy it. Solutions for difficulties must be sought for and investigated. A simple rejection of a minority desire is hardly democratic or equitable. A certain sympathy with those who look for an education that meets with the approbation of their churches is demanded when we deal with this problem. A lack of sympathy is hardly the proper approach to the issue. And it is a practical problem for many citizens, not merely Catholics.

From those who want from the general public a religious school we also have a right to expect a recognition of the realities of the situation. They must not make demands which the total community is legally, financially and psychologically unprepared to meet. A request to be heard must not be strident nor must our achieved unity be jeopardized by importunate demands on the part of minorities.

With tranquillity and amity we must reason together to see what can be done. We have wise men among us who can give us counsel and if we have goodwill we can work out better arrangements than we have.

In meetings such as this, we need the calm objectivity and goodwill of one party toward the other. Neither side has as yet come up with anything more than a doctrinaire position. The chanting of shibboleths like "separation of church and state" or "primacy of religion in the education of the child of religious parents" will not get us forward in the quest of an answer to our problem. Patient and kindly discussion for some time to come will be needed for the settlement of the conflict of interests among our citizens.

IV.

MORAL

VALUES

in AMERICAN

CULTURE

MOST boys grow up in their native city with a practical knowledge of its streets and districts. They can move from one to the other without the slightest difficulty. On foot or by bus they can travel in security with foreknowledge of their destination and of the routes by which they may arrive at it. Yet those boys may not know abstractly how the city is geographically arranged nor do they relate their own comings and goings with reference to the points of the compass. If you were to ask any one of them about different parts of the town, he could tell you how to get there from where he is standing, but he could not draw a city plan for you. He has never seen one nor would it be helpful for him in terms of his own interest.

I

All of us are like that boy in the matter called culture. By this latter word I mean the intellectual pattern which underlies the concrete arrangements for living together. In imitation of the Germans, let us call the practical, visible, material network of our artifacts, customs, styles, language, modes and tools "civilization," and the implicit intellectual vision under this network "culture." Culture and civilization are inextricably fused.

The culture makes the civilization and the civilization in turn modifies the culture. Cultures can be gradually or abruptly modified to a point where they are new things, and it is also true that with great changes in civilization, cultures yet remain substantially the same.

The influence of civilization and culture on the individual is obviously enormous. The way a man is to live is dictated immediately by the culture in which he exists. He can react against this culture, but initially the culture makes certain types of action spontaneous to the human agent. Cultural suggestions are accepted without criticism by most people living in the culture, and in many men the ways of a specific culture are unconsciously equated with the established ways of reason and nature. Such people are utterly unaware of the existence of culture and its role in life, but the great thinkers and historians of our race have perceived its reality and they have meditated on it extensively.

In America, despite diverse backgrounds and beliefs, we all live together. Hence there is here a civilization and therefore a culture. The question immediately arises if there is a specifically American culture. Arnold Toynbee would be of the opinion that there is no such thing as an American culture but only a local variant of what he would call the culture of the West. For him the cultural unit would not be the American way of life but rather the Western way, which is the basic pattern of American existence along with some accidental peculiarities of its own. Frenchmen, Englishmen, Italians, Germans and Americans would not be specifically different in their cultures, though they will manifest the one basic culture in slightly different forms. An Arab for Toynbee would be culturally distinct from an American but a Spaniard would not.

It is not for us to make this kind of distinction. We are neither historians nor sociologists. But what we can do is admit that there is an American way of life, and it matters little if this be a specific culture or an accidental variation of a culture enveloping both Americans and others.

Can we formulate articulately the substance of American culture? If it is observable, it is obviously possible to do so. However, this does not mean that every American is in a position to actuate this possibility. We are told that air is an odorless, tasteless gas. Such a description is really meaningless. Air is so pervasive in human life that it conditions every type of sensation. Perhaps to a Martian earth air might be highly odorific and pungently tasty. To an earth-man, perpetually saturated with this air, its odor is incapable of producing a recognizable sensation, for all other odors are differentiated by comparison with it. In itself it escapes significant perception. Culture is like the air we breathe. It cannot be perceived by the man in it unless he can compare it with other ambients.

Hence it is that those who travel are the ones who

understand something about their own culture because they become aware of variants with which to compare it. The traveler is visibly struck with cultural differences. The historian and student of different peoples, by means of reports from other times and places, can also note differences even if they do not travel. But the man exclusively immersed in his own culture with no windows open to other ways of life will never know what his own culture is.

Culture is never conceived by a people at some moment prior to their peoplehood. It is the soul of being a people. It forms itself invisibly without articulation as the unreflective consensus of the collectivity. We are witnessing an interesting phenomenon in the Communist countries. Here, initially, a group of strong-willed men captured control of the coercive powers residing in the community and, with these as their tool, attempted the destruction of the previous culture in order to produce an entirely new one. It is their hope that with time they will realize in their people and in the peoples of all the world their own cultural blueprints. Yet it is already evident that they will not be able to achieve their goals. Although the people on whom they work will be changed, they will also change the plans imposed on them. We are told that Chinese Communism is already different from Russian Communism, with the result that there is between the leaderships of the two countries a controversy about Communist orthodoxy. The brute fact remains that China cannot be Communist or anything else in the Russian way. The Russian people has been with us for many centuries and by its preceding cultures has been molded in such a fashion that it will react in a different fashion to the same ideas thrust on the Chinese people. Chinese and Russian civilizations can be re-formed to look much like each other, but essentially they will be different because each derives from a culture and the two cultures involved are extremely different. It is only Communist faith that foresees a substantial similarity in the two lands. And this too is indicative of all cultures; they rest on a faith.

II

What is the American faith and what are its moral consequences? This is an interesting question but it is hardly wise to expect a good answer to it. When a culture is dead, the historians perform an autopsy on it, and they can with some approximation describe the anatomy of that culture. But while a culture is alive, it is changing and it is hard to pin it down to any accurate formula. However, for the purpose of this exposition it is not necessary to give a precise description of American culture. It will be enough to indicate certain elements in it having moral relevance.

First we must get rid of a half truth. We hear often

in our time that the United States is a pluralistic society. The phrase means that there is no consensus of the American people concerning the ultimate dimensions of reality. We are supposed to be a fusion of many minorities who remain minorities in the total whole. Hence religiously we are divided up into some 250 groups with still more groups adhering to a nonreligious vision of the real. There is certainly a truth in this statement but this does not mean that in America there are, say, 260 cultures. There is only one and it derives from the consensus of the 260 groups. The groups do effectively agree on the nature of the real, otherwise they could not live together, work together, play together, fight a common foe together. There is a theology at the heart of American culture just as there is a theology at the heart of any other culture. This theology must be admitted by the mass of the people, for otherwise dynamic coexistence would be impossible. The theology is philosophical and not religious, and in America it is the kind of theology which permits different religions and nonreligious groups to exist together.

There are three great philosophical strains in American culture. The first Europeans to arrive on these shores were Protestant Englishmen. The society which they formed evolved into the present American community. The Protestants who first came were either dissidents from the Church of England or Puritan partisans of that church. There was in them all deep hostility to prelacy and there never was a bishop in the colonies. These pioneers believed in local government in church and state by which all members had a voice in the making of communal policy. They were a people dedicated to the principles of sobriety and simplicity and they believed in the values of work and personal responsibility. They took piety for granted and spontaneously but unreflectively followed substantially the moral code of medieval Europe. They tolerated no license in matters of sex, and honesty in dealings with one's neighbor was demanded. In the matter of religion they were not united but a basic Christian vision of God was the common faith of all: Congregationalists, Anglicans, Baptists, Presbyterians and even the fringe groups, Quakers and Catholics. There was therefore a moral and theological consensus and on it the distinct colonies finally united.

However, a new element in the thinking of the colonists had begun to appear just before the colonies became one nation. It was the rationalism of eighteenth century England. The intellectual leaders of the population, men like Jefferson and Franklin, were followers of the new thought. These men also believed in God but they were cold to any notion of orthodoxy concerning him or it. They did not quarrel with the churches at hand, but they made it clear that no single church was going to impose its orthodoxy as the basis of communal life.

Puritanism and rationalism working together

brought the United States to birth. In consequence a new land was opened to European immigrants of any belief or culture. The nineteenth century was a period of immigration; wave after wave of settlers came from all over Europe; from the West, the Balkans and the Levant. They built the canals, the railroads and the factories. They made the cities big. The predominant motive for their immigration was to better themselves socially and economically. In the matter of religion they were heterogeneous but by and large they had a natural faith in the possibilities of work and thrift. They were poor but they believed that this would be a passing situation. They had evolved a Puritanism of their own which complemented the Puritanism of the original English settlers.

By the end of the First World War the country was organized industrially and politically. The United States was universally recognized as a world power and the fruits of past labor and thrift became manifest. The nation had become wealthy with a singularly high standard of living common to the majority of the people, nor was there any readiness to freeze this standard of material living. Everyone wished to extend it beyond the achievement of the actual moment. The former tendency to thrift and industriousness was halted, though it did not die altogether. Yet the new air of the land was one of search for comfort rather than a whole-souled dedication to work and simplicity.

III

We see in this schematic outline three ideas basic to what we can call American culture. There is a Puritanism at the very heart of it. It is not merely the original English variety but the form proper to the later immigrants as well. There is also a rationalism churning in this puritanical matrix. Because of it orthodoxy in matters religious is suspect, but religion itself is respected provided it does not attempt to dominate the lives of the citizens. There never has been in this country any hostility to religion as such, though any concrete religion will be attacked if it tries to become a public power. Strangely enough the culture of the land expects a man to have a religion and it looks askance at the man who makes no religious profession. But it is expected that this religious affiliation should be private and moral in its concerns.

We also note an observable change in American culture since the end of the First World War. The radical Puritanism has been drastically modified. It is still respected and it is still considered the right approach to life but in practice it is withering away. The concern for comfort, luxury, amusement and physical well-being is smothering the puritan drive in our folkways. Quitting time is more important than starting time in all forms of work. Personal pride in the labor product is vanishing. The pleasure-search is keen and sexuality of an adolescent kind is coloring our national life. Yet strangely this has not driven the people from the churches. Church affiliation is higher today than ever before, and the religious trimmings on public life are now more visible than in the past. The result has been paradoxical, for we are a people who theoretically believe in Puritanism but in practice reject it.

The situation of the moment is undoubtedly dangerous. We seem to be following the pattern of past cultures in their growth and decline. We have passed through an initial period of puritanical virtue which has been highly productive of social solidarity and economic well-being. The national prosperity we have achieved has weakened the Puritanism and no effective dynamism has been substituted for it. Movement now is in terms of momentum from the past, but this momentum is gradually slowing down. The question which faces the contemporary American is whether he can bring back a puritanical drive to his national life or at least substitute for it a push just as strong.

IV

Let us consider the effects of this general situation on the life of the individual American. The consciousness of having much easily leads him to generosity, but it is the generosity of the man who loses little by his giving. In fact, the generosity itself may be an instance of prodigality. The extravagant tipper is not generous but only unconcerned and lavish. There is still much genuine generosity in the land, but it is also true that there is much generosity which is only extravagance.

Well-being is an intoxicant and it produces euphoria. In such a mood all things seem possible. There is a rosy optimism from which arises the expectation that things will continue as they are or perhaps even be better. The darker aspects of reality are ignored and honest struggling with difficult problems gives way to a confident trust that things will work out well by themselves. The girding of lean loins for battle is put off until war is already declared. Battles need trained soldiers and this training cannot be improvised. But training is hard and only some kind of Puritanism, stoic or Christian, can make it palatable. Our flight from Puritanism renders us collectively incapable of the rigors of training. The modern concern for dieting is a strange phenomenon in a world where almost two-thirds of mankind are underfed. And in our dieting we all look for a regime which will work without willpower and we want to become slim not because it will make us stronger for work and endurance but for esthetic reasons. We diet, but we do not fast.

Older American Puritanism stressed free will and personal responsibility. American Calvinism was definitely Arminian. Whatever be the deficiencies of Arminian theology, it certainly does make for strenuous effort on the part of the believer. The New England town meeting was the civic expression of this spirit. The town's business was everybody's business and all were conjointly responsible, nor did they shirk this responsibility. Today we have less faith in this kind of assembly because it has grown large and can easily be manipulated by a few men. We have become victims of a mentality which glorifies production and organization. Only specialists can understand the mechanisms that keep the social body in action. As a result we must turn over our problems to trained experts and because of it we are more than ready to let George do it. We complain of the impositions of government, but as individuals we do nothing about it because we feel that there is nothing we can do except register our discontent. We have lost the sense of responsibility for government and with it the belief that we can efficaciously influence it. Our criticisms are frustrating because they can do so little to change what they criticize.

The high esteem for personal responsibility and personal capacity in the nineteenth century produced a favorable atmosphere for the development of the great American inventors. Edison was not a learned scientist but he gave the world the phonograph and the electric light. Morse invented the telegraph. Goodrich vulcanized rubber. Many machines were devised by the men of the past century, but today it is different. Individuals can still make gadgets but revolutionary inventions need scientific training. This training supposes the discipline of the university and great things like the control of atomic energy come from university teams. Even in our schooling the individual has come to mean less than formerly. He must gear himself into a machine that produces the final product. The individual still remains an individual but his value is less individualistic. He tends to become lost in a group that is united as horses are united to the same plow but not among themselves in personal solidarity.

The only field where the individual can move at his own rhythm and on his own terms is in the realm of the spirit. He can philosophize as he pleases, though few men care to engage in the enterprise. He can also develop his religious life in terms of interiority. It is not freakish that contemporary Americans are more interested in religion than formerly. It is the only realm of concern where their freedom is ample. They cannot exercise much influence on the immense machine of government which so few understand. They cannot produce things in their own way because production is highly specialized and organized. They cannot play in their own way because sports and entertainment have become standardized by rules and conventions. Only in man's approach to God is man unhampered.

But social life is not inspired by religious concerns. Here there is a pattern at work which is autonomous

143

and free floating. The strong accent is to sell more in order to produce more and on this ascending spiral national well-being is said to depend. We do not produce what we need but we produce and then persuade men that they need the product. Society needs not only producers but also visible and hidden persuaders. Production is unrelated to need so that we have a farm surplus which is an embarrassment of riches. On this basis the puritan virtue of doing without is really a sin. To be a good citizen you must buy and not abstain from buying. Thrift, according to this principle, is a crime. Prodigality is the true virtue.

Thanks to rationalized production, we can produce goods more and more easily than ever before. The working day has not been extended because of increased production. It actually has been shortened and it will be further shortened as time goes on. Only one-fourth of a week is gainfully employed, leaving triple the time to personal initiative. However this augmented leisure has not stimulated our age to increased personal creativity. Gardens indeed are being planted and cultivated; some men have gone in for painting or for do-it-yourself work in the home. But the majority use leisure to be entertained and they use the machines which are responsible for the leisure to amuse them in this leisure time. For so large a public entertainment can only be vulgarized and even used as an instrument of persuasion rather than a stimulus to creativity. The individual is disappearing and making way for the mass man.

V

How can man be virtuous in this climate? It certainly will not be easy. Insisting always on the Christian doctrine that true virtue depends on grace which is given on God's initiative and not ours, it is still true from the Christian viewpoint that virtue is man's greatest exercise of freedom and the noblest expression of personal responsibility. There is another Christian doctrine which insists that given man's condition of Original Sin, virtue is hard and not easy even when inspired and dynamized by grace. Christian writers on the spiritual life have always laid stress on the principle that a spirit of mortification and abnegation is needed for a virtuous life. Every great moral thinker, Christian and non-Christian, has taught that great action of human significance always involves self-denial.

Our retreat from Puritanism has made mortification, abnegation and self-denial unattractive concepts. With an infantile conception of freedom we think that we are freest when in a spirit of Rousseauistic naturalism we let ourselves go in any direction toward which whim or uncontrolled instinct moves us. Surely this is not freedom in an ethical sense but sheer irresponsibility. Some control is being exercised by the social pressure of the community still living off the substance of the former puritan vision, but this substance is growing thin because more and more people have lost faith in the

145

puritan ideal. As this group increases, the saving influence of past Puritanism will be spent.

I do not know how to bring back puritanical self-denial nor do I think that it should be brought back in the form in which it existed. Nor do I know how to bring forth an efficacious substitute for it. This problem is too large for me. However, I can make a prophetic protest to the men of our day. History has shown that a culture which depersonalizes its citizens is a culture on its way to death. Such a culture accelerates its own demise. Personality is not at all the same as individuality. Cranks and eccentrics are highly individualistic but hardly deeply personal. Freedom is not only the capacity to do what we please but also the capacity to do what is called for.

Today more than ever the man in our society must make great efforts to form and strengthen his personality. This calls for the development of asceticism which means the exercise of man's power to say no to spontaneous urges of instinct. The fruit of asceticism need not be rigor or stubborn inflexibility. The ascetic does not necessarily turn down the suggestion of instinct but he will never be swept away by it. He refuses to say yes to unjudged impulse. After judgment he may well say yes, not because it is instinctive but because it is reasonable. Instinct as such is indifferent to the reasonability of its action, but it is not so structured that every instinctive desire is necessarily irrational. Man's intelligence

146

must judge in every case and asceticism makes him fit to judge.

In the day when Athens was in the height of its glory, Socrates, Plato, Aristotle and Demosthenes raised the prophetic cry to the Athenians, but as we know, it failed. However, there is nothing written in the stars that the Athenians were foredoomed to fail. The cry has its own efficacy though it does not infallibly achieve its goal. That which reduces the power of the invitation to asceticism is the difficulty of accepting it in an environment of plenty. It is not hard to practice poverty when material goods are lacking, because willy-nilly the poor are poor. For the rich poverty is much more difficult because they must do without the things which are palpably at hand. Yet even for the rich it is not impossible. Our earlier American tradition did induce the rich to live frugally because of the dynamism of the general puritan vision. The stories of John D. Rockefeller, who himself lived sparsely and raised his children to live in the same way, are well known. The display and extravagance of the rich of other countries was never considered fitting in our country and those Americans who imitated the luxuriating plutocrats in other places were judged adversely.

What is called for now is the training of our children in the ways of asceticism. This is the necessary task and it is unpopular for two reasons. The first has been with us a long time. Our parents are persuaded that their children should have more of this world's goods than the earlier generation enjoyed when they were small. The result is that no youth in history is as pampered as ours, and the fruit is juvenile delinquency. The second reason is not so old. It became popular in this century and derived from the theories of some educators who objected to ascetical training because it repressed the urges of youth. They believed that these urges should be allowed free play in order to bring out the uninhibited personality. This theory today is bombarded with widespread criticism and there is no need here to attack it anew. It is so vulnerable that one wonders how it ever won the approval of our society. The theory is no longer so dominant in the education of our children but it has not altogether disappeared.

Certainly religion can be of great assistance in inculcating asceticism. However, we must not make the serious error of thinking that it is the function of religion to save a culture. Religion is not concerned with this world's well-being. It wishes to lead man into a world beyond ours. In its own proper effort it will indeed help the secular order, but this is incidental and not the purpose of religion. The words of the Sermon on the Mount bring this out so well: "Seek first the Kingdom of God and his justice, and all of these things shall be given you besides." (Mt. 6:33)

Our contemporary culture makes much of religion, more so than was done in the past. However, modern religious concern is not deep. Affiliation with the churches grows by leaps and bounds, but an ascetical dedication to the vision of the churches is hardly the consequence. Our churches must produce figures like John the Baptist, who, in camel skin and hunger, called the world to repentance. Perhaps that figure is too dour for our time, but Francis of Assisi in winsome fashion accomplished great things in the thirteenth century.

No man can decide on his own initiative to be St. Francis. He must be called by God. But one thing Christians can do is pray the Lord to raise up in our own time the saints who will call us back to the asceticism necessary to our religious concern and our cultural necessity.

V.

The CHURCH
and the PUBLIC
CONSCIENCE

THE Church in any civil society has a dual reality. She conceives herself to be in a kingdom not of this world, and she keeps her eyes on the heavenly Jerusalem. And yet, precisely because she insists that she is a visible society, she is incorporated in the cities which were built by man. She may sigh for the other-worldly Jerusalem but her work is definitely in Paris, New York and Tokyo.

What are the obligations of the Church to the cities of men? Some believers and many nonbelievers would like to say that she has none and therefore must not meddle; but this answer is too simple. She cannot detach herself from the soil in which she is planted, even if her roots go deeper. She is not merely unworldly, but quite worldly as well. Like her Lord, she may not pray for the world, but she certainly prays in the world.

Therefore the Church has obligations to the world. In any secular situation the Church must at least give witness to the good news that in the Christ-event, salvation, has come to mankind, and that this salvation is available to all. Whether the environment be hostile or friendly, this primal obligation is pressing. It derives not from the rights of the secular community but rather from the imperative imposed on the Church by the Christ.

However, this role of the Church in secular society is not secular. It is sacral and transcends the concerns of the temporal society of men. But it is not something abstract or merely Platonic. The idea of salvation includes a way of life on earth, here and now. A way of life produces a visible comportment affecting others, and that must be a concern of the directors of the visible order of the commonwealth. The very fact of the distinction between church and state produces tension. But this tension need not induce conflict. Anode and cathode are not at war with each other. Tension can be a dynamic for heightened activity. Though this is so, and a consummation devoutly to be wished, the possibility of conflict is inherent in the basic distinction.

The Church is inevitably interested in the world because her members are necessarily citizens of the world. If the Church is interested in the whole man who is her member, she cannot be unconcerned about the worldly component of his being. She must seek first the kingdom of God and its righteousness, but that righteousness has a terrestrial *mise-en-scène*.

One obligation which has often been suggested is that the Church is the conscience of the secular community. Because this proposition seems to please many men, it will be necessary to analyze it with care. We might have a civic community, for example, in which the overwhelming majority of citizens seriously belong to one church. In such a situation, Church and civic society would be so fused that it would be difficult to say whether the community at any moment was acting as Church or as a republic.

Congregrationalist New England in the seventeenth century was so structured. The town meeting was held in the building which was both a church and a town hall. The religious dimension of the citizens was manifest in citizen action all the time. The common effort was simultaneously religious and secular. In fact, the Puritans considered their whole collectivity to be the gathered elect, whose fellowship was more of heaven than of earth. In these circumstances there cannot be the slightest doubt that the Church was the conscience of the community. It was precisely in function of that conscience that the community was formed and operated. He who did not belong to the Church had no real place in society and was treated as a transient guest or a tolerated stranger—or ejected.

It seems to me that such a community is a viable form of society, provided that circumstances in the world allow the existence of a closed collectivity. If by the nature of the interrelationships of politics, culture, science and economy a closed society is out of the question, the absolute sovereignty of the circumscribed community must relinquish some dimensions of its autonomy. It is here not a question of ideology but a matter of necessity. Whether you are for or against an open society is irrelevant when circumstances make only the open society possible. In our time the interpenetration of all human action makes a closed society in any one geographic area out of the question. It is not to the point to say that society should be open or that it should not be. It is simply a fact that it is. Obviously this openness admits of degrees, and it will not be identical in every place.

In such a situation, in what sense can the Church be the conscience of the community? First of all, it must be recognized that the world visions functioning in the citizens of any current particular society are not one but many. The open society is pluralistic. In consequence, there will be some citizens who feel no concern for religion, while others are sincerely attached to religious values. Nor will all the religious citizens belong to one church; some will belong to none. There will be many churches, and the Church will be a shorthand symbol for religion insofar as it is active in the community. Even if one church is by law established, as is the case with the Church of England, the religious influence on the nation cannot be identified exclusively with that church. The nonconformists and the free churches are also included under the term "Church."

If we understand "Church" in this large sense, is it meaningful to call the Church the conscience of the nation? Certainly not, if a large portion of the citizenry is not religiously concerned. This may be the case in Russia. The available facts are so confusing that it is difficult to decide. It is well to remember that genuine Communist ideology has nothing to say about God, nor does it wish to prove that there is no God. It merely considers the whole issue to be irrelevant. The unreality of a divine being is postulated, and in consequence religion, because it distracts man from his proper creative action, is declared baneful.

The Communists do admit the reality of an absolute—matter evolving according to a dialectic; but since this is not spiritual, no religion can be derived from it. Yet religion is tolerated in Communist countries, provided it is purely internal and does not interfere with the activities of the socialistically organized community. This toleration is justified by the system on the grounds of the evolutionary process in society. Religion is a historical fact prior to Communist control, and when Communism takes over, it finds religion there as a residue of an earlier stage of evolution which will be transcended automatically as socialism continues. Religion will inevitably wither away, and there is no call to use violence against it.

Communist theory will not permit the Church to be the conscience of the united people. Yet one of the weaknesses of any government which tries to operate rigorously by a blueprint based on a priori postulates is that facts may ignore the a priori. Poland is a Communist state, and the Church there may well be the conscience of the people, government notwithstanding. *De jure* the Church can have no influence on public life, but *de facto* it can be very important indeed.

The Communist situation is not universal. In the

greater part of the world the state is not opposed to religion. Communist hostility to it helps to produce an opposite reaction in the states which feel themselves threatened by the Reds. The Russian astronaut, Yuri Gagarin, found no god in space, but the American, John Glenn, set out for space in a prayerful mood. What is the role of religion in a commonwealth like America?

First of all, the American Constitution, bolstered strongly by the American tradition, demands the separation of church and state. But as has been pointed out in the Supreme Court, the American tradition never separated public life from religion. The resulting situation is inevitably paradoxical. The institutionalized corporations of religion have no privilege in American public law, but since the corporations are religious, they indirectly enjoy the general goodwill toward religion. The armed forces have chaplains who are always commissioned officers. Chapels exist in most of the army, navy and air force centers. These chapels are all supplied and maintained by the republic. Civic events and even political rallies begin and end with prayer by a clergyman.

Church properties, owned by institutionalized societies, are exempt from tax. This consideration is always directed toward religion and never to its privately organized societies in their distinct individuality. The Church, if understood exclusively as generic visible religious action, is palpably privileged in America, but Church, if understood as a specifically structured particular community, is always treated in law with nervous aloofness.

In America, is the Church, no matter how you understand the term, the public conscience? Certainly there is no explicit or implicit contract existing between Church and general society to this effect. Neither in law nor in fact is religion an ultimate norm whereby legislators, executives, or judges go about their tasks. No court would accept a plea based on the illegality of a statute because of its violation of some religious principle, though the courts do accept pleas based on the claim that certain legislation or governmental action deprives the citizen of his recognized right to be religious. In this country religion is considered a private thing producing a public fact; religion precisely as such has no juridical standing, though the religious fact is admittedly relevant to public policy.

Religion, then, cannot be the official conscience of this land. Is it in fact the moral guide of the people? Americans think that religion is bigger than any church and bigger than the sum total of churches. A natural religiosity, which functions without much reference to the individual churches, does operate in many citizens who are unaffiliated with any existing church society or whose affiliation is only nominal. This kind of religiosity goes no further than recognition of a Supreme Being.

If we consider the individual churches, the organized fellowships with a definable doctrine and practice, we run into a dismaying phenomenon. There are more than 250 sects and denominations in the land, and they are all different. The unity of God means something quite different to Unitarians, Jews, Lutherans and Catholics. The moral code held by each separate religious community can reductively be unified, but the consistent particular believer wants no such reduction.

We must certainly admit that each church has the civil right and the obligation to teach and demand a code of behavior for those who are in its union. If it does not do this, it is obviously unfaithful to its own mission. Those outside the membership may consider the moral directives given unfortunate or unreasonable, but if the teaching shows no clear and present danger of undermining the common good, they must in the spirit of political freedom respect the rights of the fellowship, which is a free union of free citizens.

When the individual church urges certain norms of conduct on its members with the penalty of expelling the nonconforming member, it is acting according to its civil rights. Its action cannot be a valid concern for those outside the fellowship. Outsiders are free to form and voice their disagreement with the church in question, but they cannot suppress its right to teach its own free constituency. Suppression violates the guaranteed freedom of the citizen. If there should be a general hostility directed toward a particular church, this fact will inhibit the church in its action, but the inhibition derives from a fact and not from any legal infringement of right.

But a church's civil right goes beyond the confines of its own closed fellowship. Its members, singly or together, can urgently propose their specific vision of life and reality to the community at large. A single man or a group of men can speak their minds to the whole body politic. They can try to convince and persuade others of the rightness of their views or of a program of action deriving from such views. The only restriction placed on this right is that the arguments must be fair. Offensive and annoying proselytizing, slanderous attacks on others, lobbying for power and the abuse of legal technicalities in order to favor partisan programs are unfair. In the popular mind, no church has the right to use such means. But that it should speak its mind in public with the intention of enlisting the support of the community is in principle, if not always in fact, welcomed by the citizenry. This welcome derives from a general, though not universal, conviction that all who have worthwhile insights for the common welfare should make them known. However, the community wants such ideas proposed, not imposed. The republic will decide; it refuses to have decisions made for it.

Is the Church—understood as one church, or the totality of all churches or religion in general—in fact the conscience of the commonwealth? Realism makes us tend to say no. In our kind of democracy, neither in law nor in fact does the community give the Church the right to be the arbiter of the nation's ethics. There is a common belief that the Church's word is relevant to civic concern, but although the Church is one of the genuine factors that help to form conscience, it is not the sole factor.

There are two different groups present in our country. The first group, in its strong adherence to religion, thinks that some definite religious dogma is binding in conscience on all Americans. We hear from time to time the phrase: "After all, America is a Christian nation." This statement is ambiguous. If no more is meant than the statistical fact that the majority of citizens claim to be Christian in their religious commitments, be these strong or weak, the statement is true but hardly to the point. If the statement wishes to insinuate that the American is somehow bound in conscience to accept certain Christian dogmas as directive of our national life, it is false.

A second group operating in our midst is anti-religious. Since there can be no religious test in our way of life, these men and women are genuinely and validly citizens no less than the Americans who are believers. Our laws and our tradition do not demand that they be converted. Yet such men and women must not confuse two different ideas. Separation of church and state does not mean the relegation of religion to the invisible recesses of the human heart. The American idea is rather that religion has a public function. It must speak out, and it must be heard, though its voice is not necessarily decisive. It can be decisive only when the people as a whole accept definite religious guidance, but even then it is decisive only because the people will it, not because of any religious premise involved in their achievement of the decision.

In the American scheme, the republic cannot impose a religious obligation on any citizen. The opponent of religion has the right to protest any governmental pressure exerted on him in order to make him engage in a religious act. But he has no right to protest when the government acts to foster the relevance of religion to the national existence. Separation of church and state in Russia means the complete and utter irrelevance of religion to communal life. Separation of church and state in the United States implies the relevance of religion but grants it no juridical authority. Relevance will be protected; church domination will be resisted.

Since no moral vision can be legislated, and yet morality is so relevant to legislation, the spontaneous moral consensus of the people as a whole is very important. This consensus is a fact, and different influences combine to make it real. Groups can use propaganda shrewdly and effectively to produce a consensus; tyranny, if it endures for a long time and uses collective brainwashing, can induce a precarious consensus. However, the consensus is the flower of human freedom; it is not the fruit of a legislator's fiat or dictator's club. Even the legal formulas of past consensus cannot override its present shape and autonomy. The consensus which operates is a living thing in the now. The past helped to form it, but the present gives it its being.

Nor are we dealing with ephemeral cults, fads, modes and movements. These are superficial; their action is not profound. Moral consensus is the public philosophy of a community, which is there just as the weather is there. You may not like it; you may want to change it; but you will also have to resign yourself to the fact of its existence. It is the public philosophy which people use in their collective interactions without having achieved it by any philosophic method. It is common sense, which, even when it is not conspicuous as sense, is undeniably common. It takes a keen observer to find its essence, because it is not reflective, nor are its principles necessarily verbalized or its consequences articulated.

It is this commonly felt conviction which makes the society alive. The laws do not make it, but it gives the precise meaning of law. Law can function only to the degree that consensus gives it energy. Where consensus embraces a vast area of public concern, written laws are not necessary, because the living common will does easily and simply what complicated laws could achieve only inefficiently. It is this consensus of the people which is truly the conscience of the nation.

One might ask whether consensus is really a national fact. The answer is that its truth is inescapable. Men and women do collaborate in a given area; they do live together; they do interlace their existences one with the other. Not every single individual in the community will subscribe to the consensus, but when a predominant majority of the people do subscribe to an opinion, the consensus becomes clearly defined. The wider the moral area of consensus, the greater will be the harmony of national life. Even when the area is not very large, there must always be a minimal consensus on basic moral issues, permitting collaboration and living together. That there are not more murders in our land is due not merely to the efficiency of our police. There are small communities where, practically speaking, there is no police force, and yet there are no murders at all. The American people by consensus reject murder because they believe it is inadmissible. This, rather than any written decree in the statutes, is what ultimately outlaws murder. The average American cannot philosophize about murder, but he certainly is against it, and in no uncertain terms. This is not merely an individual stand; it is a common persuasion, operating as the social will rather than as the consequence of adding up a large number of individual wills. That is consensus.

We are faced by two great problems in the matter of our American consensus. The first is that its area is small and constantly shrinking. As a result, there is no effective general guidance for our young people and for our morally obtuse citizens. Honesty, sobriety, industriousness, self-reliance and regard for the neighbor's personal dignity certainly were elements in the American consensus of the past. I wonder just how much is left of these moral ideals in the actual consensus of our day. They certainly have not disappeared altogether, but obviously they are much thinner than they were. In the past, religious morality helped to make these factors strong in our consensus. The attraction of church laws is weak today, and they do not function as they did in the past.

Yet the relaxation of moral bonds is hurting us. We speak of our vacillating sense of national purpose. The government is searching for morale builders and boosters. Everywhere we hear complaints that the public schools have failed to teach moral principles. Actually, the present consensus is not sturdy enough to communicate a healthy moral framework for our national existence. The signs are without number: work-shirking, evasion of obligation, sloppy craftsmanship, shrill demands for pleasure and comfort, scorn for asceticism, uninhibited sensual and sexual indulgence, hostility to obedience and the oblivion of communal responsibility. These things are never altogether absent in any society, but they are dismayingly visible in our own.

What can we rationally and democratically do about our inadequate consensus? One solution offered by many good men is to urge the people to go to church. We see advertisements in buses and on billboards attempting to do so. Yet there are enough arguments to make us doubt the efficacy of this tactic. It is not that widespread religious commitment could not better our situation, but rather that in principle it would be no solution.

I should like to make a tentative suggestion. I should like to see our pundits of the press and on the campus investigate once more the idea that morality is structured objectively no less than the human body. If it is, just as medical scientists can draw up rules for bodily health, so our moralists could set forth rules for our public philosophy. In a discourse of reason, which is the universal possession of all men, no matter what their attitudes toward religion may be, a reasonable moral code can be proposed persuasively to the whole commonwealth.

The reader will smile and say that I am trying to bring back the notion of natural law. Of course that is what I am doing—but with a variation. Too long have defenders of natural law supposed that this concept was either a mystical achievement or a rational discovery of a complete code written somewhere in the Platonic sky. The mystic found it without critical research, written in the fleshy tablets of the heart. The a priori Platonist thought it was something that could be deduced to the last detail with mathematical rigor. Neither way seems helpful in our predicament. The mystic appeals to a vision that is not available to the commonality of men, and the rationalistic deontologist is too far removed from the empirical realities of existence.

But a rule of reason can be established without adopting either of these positions. Reason does achieve reality—metaphysical, physical and moral. The technician accepts what the physicist says about iron, and he will not use it in a way counter to its structure. Iron can be employed to satisfy human needs. The physical, psychological, sociological and spiritual factors in men can be and are being studied. The moralist, who is a kind of technician, can study the human structure and the human environment. He can, in terms of sound inference from right reason, construct a practical code for human action. We do not expect a perfect scheme from such thought. Let it be adequate only for our needs, and let its principles be open to a discussion based on sound premises. A scheme so formed will not be a once-for-all achievement. The changes that constantly modify our environment will demand new codes. This is not an affirmation of relativism, but it is a plea for relevance.

The Church is not the conscience of the American community, though it plays an influential role in the formation of such a conscience. The conscience itself is the consensus of the nation. This consensus will not be healthy unless it is constantly put under the searching light of the criticism of the qualified observers of the national scene. To be a qualified observer one must be a moral philosopher working on rational principles, rather than on mystical intuitions or sheerly pragmatic assumptions. Morality is a structure of its own, utterly real and true to intrinsic principles of abiding applicability.